GREAT AMERICAN VACATIONS

by Robert D. Blashek

©1988 VENTURA ASSOCIATES, INC.
PRINTED IN THE UNITED STATES.
ALL RIGHTS RESERVED.
THIS BOOK MAY NOT BE REPRODUCED
IN WHOLE OR IN PART OR IN ANY
FORM OR FORMAT WITHOUT WRITTEN
PERMISSION OF THE PUBLISHER.
VENTURA ASSOCIATES, INC.
1350 AVENUE OF THE AMERICAS
NEW YORK, NY 10019

Acknowledgments

Thank you to Richard Parisi, President of Great American Magazines, whose sponsorship makes publication of this book possible.

Also many thanks to the Bureaus of Travel and Tourism of all the States, whose cooperation in providing up-to-date material was extremely valuable.

And a special thanks to Linda Schupack, whose charm and wit are reflected in this guide, making it interesting and fun to read.

Travel Intro

Vacation time is nearing, and you've decided to see the States. There's so much to see out there that it's hard to know where to begin. New England? The South? The Southwest? The Midwest? The Pacific Northwest?

This is the first question you'll have to answer in planning your vacation. Of course, the amount of time you have to spend may influence where you'll be going. The more time, certainly, the more you can see—but that's not to say you can't get a fine feeling for New England in a week, or even a couple of days. And most of the individual attractions themselves require only a day's (or an afternoon's) commitment.

It's important also to think about what time of the year you want to visit these states. Most of the attractions in this book are open year round, but some of the festivals are held during very specific time periods each year. Other states are open only during specific seasons—or may have reduced hours during the off-season. Check ahead just to make sure.

The time of year becomes important for the weather you'll meet while travelling. There's nothing more lovely than autumn in Vermont—unless, of course, it's a white Christmas. But, be forewarned, they're two very, very different experiences. Similarly, the hikes you'd take in

Yellowstone in the spring or summer will take on a slightly different tenor from those embarked on during the winter months.

From the Antietam National Battlefield in Maryland to the Birmingham Zoo in Alabama, there's a whole library of experiences to choose from. If you're looking for National Parks or Seashores, they are well represented in this book. Whether it's the Grand Canyon in Arizona or Glacier Bay in Alaska or Rehoboth Beach in Delaware, there are many opportunities to revel at the spectacular beauty of both land and sea.

If a sense of history is what you are seeking, why not begin at Plimoth Plantation in Massachusetts? See the Lincoln Home in Illinois, the Henry Ford Museum in Michigan, Independence Park in Pennsylvania, Mount Rushmore in South Dakota, and don't forget the Alamo when visiting Texas.

For sheer entertainment, what better place than Disneyworld in Florida or Las Vegas (which is just a big theme park for adults) in Nevada? If you're a movie buff, the Universal Studios Tour in California is a must; and so is Graceland when visiting Tennessee. Classical music lovers should plan on attending a symphony at Tanglewood in Massachusetts.

Each state has its own regional festivals and special events. Some of the more noteworthy include the St. Paul Winter Festival in Minnesota, NEBRASKAland Days in—you guessed it—Nebraska, the Norsk Hostfest in North Dakota, and the Johnny Appleseed Festival in Indiana. Most of these events occur around the same time each year—but it's still better to confirm the date than schedule a whole vacation around the

Cowboy Poetry Reading in Nevada only to discover the readings will occur a month later this year.

With sports being America's national pastime, there are opportunities both to participate and to pay homage. The Baseball Hall of Fame in New York is at the top of any fan's list, as is Churchill Downs in Kentucky. The Pro-Football Hall of Fame in Ohio is a key maneuver for Sunday afternoon arm-chair quarterbacks, too. Those desiring a bit more physical activity will find it white water rafting in Idaho or skiing the Green Mountains of Vermont.

If shopping (and snacking) is part of the game plan, Harborplace in Maryland and Faneuil Hall in Massachusetts should definitely be on the list. The same goes for Country Club Plaza in Missouri.

This book provides a taste of what's out there, a sampling of the treats America offers. There's lots to see and lots to do. Use the book as a springboard to jump into your own trip. Remember to plan ahead, but more importantly, just plan on having fun.

The book provides a general introduction to travelling in the United States by featuring three exciting tourist attractions in each of the fifty states. If you're looking for more activities in a particular area, it's a good idea to consult a guidebook for that specific locale. For more details on any one of the sights listed in this book, contact the place direction. Addresses and telephone numbers are generally listed at the bottom of the description. You can also contact the state bureau of travel and tourism.

Table of Contents

INTRODUCTION ... 5

ALABAMA
Alabama Space and Rocket Center ... 16
Birmingham Zoo ... 17
Tuskegee Institute ... 17

ALASKA
Glacier Bay National Park ... 19
Denali National Park and Preserves ... 19
Pribilof Islands ... 20

ARIZONA
Grand Canyon ... 21
Monument Valley ... 21
Hoover Dam ... 22

ARKANSAS
Ozark Folk Center ... 24
Eureka Springs ... 24
Crater of Diamonds State Park ... 25

CALIFORNIA
Disneyland ... 26
Universal Studios Tour ... 26
Monterey Bay Aquarium ... 27

COLORADO
- Vail ... 28
- Garden of the Gods ... 28
- Pike's Peak ... 29

CONNECTICUT
- Wadsworth Atheneum ... 30
- Mystic Marine Life Aquarium and Seaport Museum ... 30
- Yale University ... 31

DELAWARE
- Rehoboth Beach ... 33
- Winterthur ... 33
- Hagley Museum ... 34

FLORIDA
- Ringling Museums ... 35
- St. Augustine City ... 36
- Disneyworld ... 36

GEORGIA
- Cherry Blossom Festival ... 38
- Stone Mountain Park ... 38
- Six Flags Over Georgia ... 39

HAWAII
- Diamond Head/Waikiki ... 40
- Haleakala Crater ... 40
- St. Benedict's/Star of the Sea ... 41

IDAHO
- Sun Valley ... 42
- National Old Time Fiddle Contest ... 43
- White Water Rafting ... 43

ILLINOIS
Sears Tower	45
Lincoln Home	45
Shawnee National Forest	46

INDIANA
Covered Bridge Festival	47
Johnny Appleseed Festival	47
Circus City	48

IOWA
Amana Colonies	49
Terrace Hill	49
Mississippi Belle/Spirit of Dubuque	50

KANSAS
Little House on the Prairie	52
International Pancake Race	52
The Eisenhower Center	53

KENTUCKY
Kentucky Derby/Churchill Downs	54
Fort Knox	54
Cumberland Falls State Park	55

LOUISIANA
Oak Alley Plantation	57
Delta Queen	57
Superdome	58

MAINE
Acadia National Park	59
Lumberman's Museum	59
L.L. Bean Store	60

MARYLAND
Historic St. Mary's City   62
Assateague State and National
Seashore Park   62
Antietam National Battlefield   63

MASSACHUSETTS
Plimoth Plantation   64
Tanglewood   64
Faneuil Hall   65

MICHIGAN
Henry Ford Museum and Greenville Village   67
Mackinac Island   68
Tulip Time Festival   68

MINNESOTA
Itasca State Park/Great River Road   70
Winter Carnival   70
Hill Annex Mine Tour   71

MISSISSIPPI
Jimmie Rodgers Museum   72
Gulf Coast   72
Natchez Trace   73

MISSOURI
Gateway Arch   74
Silver Dollar City   74
Country Club Plaza   75

MONTANA
Glacier National Park   76
Custer Battlefield National Monument   76
Yellowstone National Park   77

NEBRASKA
- Boys Town — 78
- NEBRASKAland Days — 79
- State Capitol — 79

NEVADA
- Las Vegas Strip — 81
- Cowboy Poetry Reading — 82
- Reno National Air Races — 82

NEW HAMPSHIRE
- Strawberry Banke — 84
- Mt. Washington Cog Railway — 84
- The Flume — 85

NEW JERSEY
- Cape May Beaches — 87
- Atlantic City — 87
- Washington Crossing State Park — 88

NEW MEXICO
- International Balloon Fiesta — 89
- Turquoise Trail — 89
- Indian Pueblo Cultural Center — 90

NEW YORK
- Niagara Falls — 92
- Cooperstown — 92
- New York City — 93

NORTH CAROLINA
- Cape Hatteras National Seashore — 95
- Blue Ridge Parkway — 95
- North Carolina State Government Complex — 96

NORTH DAKOTA
- Theodore Roosevelt National Park — 98
- Norsk Hostfest — 98
- North Dakota State Fair — 99

OHIO
- Pro-Football Hall of Fame — 100
- Air Force Museum — 100
- Sea World — 101

OKLAHOMA
- Discoveryland's OKLAHOMA — 102
- Will Rogers Memorial — 102
- The State Fair of Oklahoma — 103

OREGON
- Oregon Shakespearean Festival — 104
- Washington Park — 105
- Mt. Hood National Forest — 105

PENNSYLVANIA
- Independence National Historical Park — 107
- White River Rafting — 108
- Springs Folk Festival — 108

RHODE ISLAND
- Hammersmith Farm — 109
- Blithewold Gardens and Arboretum — 109
- Block Island — 110

SOUTH CAROLINA
- Myrtle Beach — 112
- Fort Moultrie/Fort Sumter — 113
- McKissick Museums — 114

SOUTH DAKOTA
- Mount Rushmore — 115
- Badlands National Park — 115
- Custer State Park — 116

TENNESSEE
- Graceland — 118
- Opryland — 119
- Great Smoky Mountains National Park — 119

TEXAS
- Alamo — 121
- Big Bend National Park — 121
- Padre Island — 122

UTAH
- Bryce Canyon National Park — 124
- Rainbow Bridge National Monument — 124
- Park City Ski Area — 125

VERMONT
- Shelburne Museum — 126
- Fall Foliage — 127
- Skiing/Green Mountains — 127

VIRGINIA
- Virginia Beach — 129
- Colonial Williamsburg — 129
- Mount Vernon — 130

WASHINGTON
- Puget Sound Ferry — 131
- Mount St. Helens — 131
- Museum of History and Industry — 132

WASHINGTON, D.C.
- National Air and Space Museum — 133
- Washington Monument — 133
- U.S. Capitol — 134

WEST VIRGINIA
- Harper's Ferry National Historic Park — 135
- New River Gorge Bridge — 135
- Canaan Valley Resort State Park — 136

WISCONSIN
- House on the Rock — 137
- EAA's Fly-In — 137
- Wisconsin Dells — 138

WYOMING
- Grand Teton National Park — 139
- Cheyenne Frontier Days — 139
- Fort Laramie — 140

INDEX — 142

Alabama

Alabama Space & Rocket Center
Dubbed the "Earth's Largest Space Museum," the Alabama Space & Rocket Center celebrates man's exploration of space. Three separate exhibits—including a hands-on simulation, a visit to an actual space lab, and a spectacular widescreen movie—round out the visitor's space experience.

The Alabama Space & Rocket Center has more than 60 astronaut-related exhibits that allow you to feel as if you're actually on the Space Shuttle or on an Apollo trip to the moon. The sights, sounds, and gravity forces are all authentic.

You can also tour the NASA-Marshall Space Flight Center and observe four labs where scientists are developing future plans for the nation's next forays into space. Another highlight of the center is its Spacedome, a theater featuring a vast 67-foot screen that makes the audience feel as if it has just been launched into space.

The center is located in Huntsville, 15 miles east of I-65 on Ala. 20. It is open daily, year-round. Camping is available nearby. For more information, contact the State of Alabama Bureau of Tourism and Travel, 532 South Perry Street, Montgomery, Alabama, 36130. You can call (800) ALABAMA.

Birmingham Zoo

The largest zoo in the seven southeastern states, the Birmingham Zoo is a must see for animal lovers. The zoological park is home to more than 750 birds, animals and reptiles—both regional and rare.

Siberian tigers, gorillas, polar bears and giraffes are just some of the animals into whose world visitors may enter. Recently, the zoo has opened an outstanding exhibit of predatory animals. If younger children need to take a rest, there is a children's train available to take them around the park.

The zoo is open daily. It is located at 2630 Cahaba Road in Birmingham. For more information, contact the State of Alabama Bureau of Tourism and Travel, 532 South Perry Street, Montgomery, Alabama, 36130. Call (800) ALABAMA.

Tuskegee Institute National Historic Site

The Tuskegee Institute contains 2 important buildings honoring George Washington Carver and Booker T. Washington. The Carver Museum celebrates the life and achievements of Dr. Carver, while the Oaks is the restored house of Booker T. Washington.

The Carver Museum contains such personal effects of Dr. Carver as paintings and needlework. It also includes exhibits of vegetables and products derived from the peanut and sweet potato, research work with which Carver was much concerned during his lifetime.

Tuskegee students built Booker T. Washington's house that was designed by the architect Robert Taylor. Washington's house takes on even greater historical significance for it is one of the few remaining houses of this period that black people have both designed and built.

Tuskegee Institute is located in Tuskegee, Alabama and is open daily. For more information contact the State of Alabama Bureau of Tourism and Travel, 532 South Perry Street, Montgomery, Alabama, 36130. You can call (800) ALABAMA.

Alaska

Glacier Bay National Park

Glaciers are probably the number one reason why people visit Alaska, and Glacier Bay National Park does not disappoint. Sixteen glaciers feed the bay and its inlets. The glaciers date back to the Pleistocene Age, approximately 10,000 years ago.

The vistas that you view hiking in the park are simply spectacular. The colors are especially striking since glaciers absorb all but blue light, making their hues an exquisite sapphire color. Set these glaciers against the scarlet flowered hills and snow-capped mountains, and the brilliance of the vision is with you forever.

The National Park Service offers daily programs from Barlett's Cove where the Visitor's Center is located. The area is also noted for its whale and bird-watching opportunities.

For more information, contact the Alaska State Division of Tourism, Pouch E-800, Juneau, Alaska, 99811, (907) 465-2010.

Denali National Park and Preserve

Denali National Park and Preserve was created around Mt. McKinley, and nearby Denali State Park offers tremendous views of this spectacular mountain.

If you want to stay in Denali, you have your

choice of hotels, hostels, or campgrounds. There is very easy access from the Park to Anchorage— either by highway or railroad. The Park Service runs informational programs daily.

While all of Alaska can see the Aurora Borealis during the fall and winter, it is particularly spectacular at Denali. Denali is also known for its great population of caribou, migrating across the tundra. For more information, contact the Alaska State Division of Tourism, Pouch E-800, Juneau, Alaska, 99811, (907) 465-2010.

Pribilof Islands

A tiny group of islands in the Bering Sea, the Pribilof Islands are breeding grounds for the northern fur seals and shorebirds. Each summer, these creatures come from various parts of the world to bear and raise their babies.

Tourists can fly from Anchorage to the Pribilof Islands where they can then view the seal and bird rockeries. Overnight accommodations are found at St. George or St. Paul, the site of a century old Russian Orthodox Church.

For more information on the Pribilof Islands, contact the Alaska State Division of Tourism, Pouch E-800, Juneau, Alaska, 99811, (907) 465-2010.

Arizona

Grand Canyon National Park

When you visit Arizona, you must spend some time at the Grand Canyon, one of America's most breath-taking sites. Though no one knows precisely when and how the Canyon was formed, it is a spectacular mile deep gorge, surrounded by magnificent rock formations whose striations change hue as they bask in the rising sun. A forest of ponderosa pine ring the Canyon's edge.

One can experience the Grand Canyon in a variety of ways: hiking, river rafting, and mule riding. For the consummate overview of the Canyon, think about a helicopter or fixed-wing aircraft tour. Each way of seeing the Canyon offers special details, shading the Canyon experience with its own particular colors.

Most of the Canyon is open all year round, although the North Rim is closed in the winter, November through April. Most of the campgrounds require reservations, especially in the summer. For more information on the Canyon, you can request information on camping and campgrounds from the Arizona Office of Tourism.

Monument Valley

Monument Valley offers a view of what the Southwest looked like hundreds of years ago, before European explorers set foot on the land. True Indian country, Arizona was called "the Land of Room and Time Enough" by its native American inhabitants. Monument Valley gets its name from the towering stone monuments that rise from the baked earth plains.

Many traditional Indian homes pepper this area also. There are two types of shelter—the log and earthen Navajo hogans located at the foot of the massive rock formations and the Hopi pueblo villages that can be found across the three mesas of the Colorado plateau.

The Navajo National Monument contains extraordinary Indian cliff dwellings, the 13th century Navajo ruins of Betakin and Keet Seel. The sprawling Navajo Reservation rings the land of the Hopi Indians and the three main mesas of the Colorado plateau. Historians believe that Oraibi, one of the Hopi villages, has had an active community longer than any other village in North America, dating it back to 1200 A.D.

The Hopis living on the First Mesa of the Colorado plateau have a reputation for creating exquisite pottery, those living on the Second Mesa produce beautiful coiled baskets, and those of the Third Mesa are noted for their wicker baskets. All work is for sale at the Hopi Cultural Center on the Second Mesa.

A brochure entitled "Indian Country Guide" is available from the Arizona Office of Tourism.

Hoover Dam

The Hoover Dam, located at the Western corner of Arizona, blocks off the 115 mile long Lake Mead from the Colorado River. The Colorado

River determines Arizona's western border and runs from the Hoover Dam down to Mexico.

This 727 foot structure holds the record as the highest concrete dam in the United States. Recognized as one of the greatest feats of engineering, it was the biggest Federal Reclamation project during the rebuilding of America's infrastructure in the 30's. Tours are available year round.

For more information on any of Arizona's attractions, contact the Arizona Office of Tourism, 1480 East Bethany Home Road, Phoenix, Arizona, 85014, (602) 255-3618.

Arkansas

Ozark Folk Center

The Ozark Folk Center, an Arkansas State Park, is a testament to the traditional life of the Ozark Mountain region. Music, crafts, songs, dance, humor—all the hallmarks of Ozark life are celebrated here.

During the day, artisans skilled in the materials and tools of 1820-1920 demonstrate the crafts of that same period. There are over 20 original stone and cedar Craft Demonstration Buildings where one can watch crafts people recreate Ozark daily life—caning chairs, milling flour, making furniture, weaving baskets, and quilting.

At night, there are musical presentations, where musicians play traditional instruments and sing songs whose lyrics reflect both the good times and bad times of Ozark existence. Special workshops on the hammered dulcimer, the autoharp, and folk dancing are also available during the season, which runs from April through October. A Fiddler's Jamboree caps off the year.

For more information, contact the Ozark Folk Center, Mountain View, Arkansas, 72560 (501) 269-3851.

Eureka Springs

This enchanting Victorian village was founded as a health resort in 1879 because of the 63 natural springs, all thought to have special curative powers. One spring, in particular, is known in Indian legends as "Great Healing Spring."

The downtown is listed as a national historic district, preserving Eureka Spring's Gay Nineties heritage. The town keeps its ties to the past, as the trolley car is the most popular way to get around. The old Eureka Springs and North Arkansas steam railway is another attraction.

The Great Passion Play—staged from May through October—also brings visitors to Eureka Springs, as does the Spring Folk Festival and Fiddle Contest.

You can get more information from the Eureka Springs Chamber of Commerce.

Crater of Diamonds State Park

Located in Murfreesboro, the Crater of Diamonds State Park is the only diamond area in North America where people can hunt for precious gems *and* keep what they find!

An old volcanic pipe called "The Crater" is the site of more than 60,000 diamond discoveries. Each year, people find another 1000 or so diamonds. While diamonds are the prime lure, people have stumbled upon other semi-precious stones like jasper, quartz, calcite, and barite.

The park also offers a visitor's center with special exhibits, a campground, and small restaurant. For more information, you can write or call: Superintendent, Crater of Diamonds State Park, Route 1, Box 364, Murfreesboro, Arkansas, 71958.

If you want details on other Arkansas attractions, write the Arkansas Department of Parks and Tourism, One Capitol Mall, Little Rock, Arkansas, 72201.

California

Disneyland

How can you come to southern California and not say hello to Mickey Mouse and Company? Open all year round, Disneyland has been around more than 30 years and is probably California's most popular attraction. Whatever time of year you visit, plan on arriving early as a full day of activities awaits you. Keep in mind that crowds are less, however, off-season.

The Pirates of Caribbean and Space Mountain rides are generally considered to be Disneyland's best, although the Matterhorn is pretty spectacular as well. One admission fee gets you in to all the rides, but arcade game costs are extra. During the summer months, there's lots of evening entertainment, the perfect nightcap to a wonderful day.

Disneyland is located in Anaheim, California, an easy car trip from Los Angeles.

Universal Studios Tours

Hooray for Hollywood. To give its visitors a taste of what goes on behind the scenes at a movie and television studio, Universal offers both a through-the-lot tram ride and special shows featuring the studio's work. The three-hour tram takes its riders through the cream of Universal's special effects—space attacks, Red

Sea flash floods, toppling bridges, killer sharks, and the Doomed Glacier ice tunnel. Of the shows, the Conan Show and the Stunt Show are most highly recommended.

You can take the Universal Tour any time during the year. If you plan on coming during the summer months, arrive before 9 a.m. or after 4 p.m. to avoid standing in line.

Universal Studios is located in Universal City.

Monterey Bay Aquarium

Barely open 3 years, the Monterey Bay Aquarium is, perhaps, the newest and largest aquarium in the world. The facility is spectacular and only enhanced by its exquisite setting in majestic Monterey. The giant kelp forest is noteworthy as are the adorable sea otters. If your schedule allows it, check out the early sea otter feeding show. The Aquarium also has many creative and educative hands-on exhibits on marine life.

Not surprisingly, weekends are extremely crowded, making mid-week an ideal time to visit.

For more information on any California attractions, contact the California Office of Tourism, 1121 L Street, Suite 103, Sacramento, California, (916) 322-1396.

Colorado

Vail

In the winter, skiers from all over the world flock to Vail where the snow lasts until well into April. Colorado skiing is known for its light, fluffy, dry powder—a skier's nirvana. The Back Bowls at Vail, where the runs last nearly forever, challenge even the most advanced skier. Vail has over 10 square miles of ski runs that offer a variety of skiing experiences to skiers of all levels.

Vail's winter festival, Winterfaire, attracts an international crowd interested in celebrating skiing in January. Throughout the season, Vail is host to several World Cup ski races as well.

The Vail gondola transports skiers more than 10,000 feet up the mountain in the summer; tourists can ride it to take advantage of the tremendous view of the Rockies that Vail's summit affords. Summertime at Vail offers everything a resort should—tennis, golf, hiking, biking, fishing, horseback riding—all in the midst of Vail's lush mountain verdure.

For more information, contact: Vail Resort Association, 241 East Meadow Drive, Vail, CO, 81657, (303) 476-1000.

Garden of the Gods

The Garden of the Gods is a 700 acre landmass marked by huge towers of red sandstone rocks that are more than 250,000,000 years old. What makes these rock formations so spectacularly enchanting, however, is the legend behind them. According to Ute Indian lore, the Great Manitou lived in Pike's Peak, a mountain visible in the distance. When giants moseyed into Ute land, the Great Manitou turned these unwelcome creatures into stone.

Many of the formations have garnered their own nicknames. If you stand at just the right angle, you can see why Vulcan's Anvil, The Three Graces, The Two Old Maids, and The Balanced Rock are thusly called.

A must, when paying homage to the Garden of the Gods, is to position yourself so that two of the rock formations frame Pike's Peak. It's a classic composition for a photograph.

Pike's Peak

Colorado has 55 mountains with peaks higher than 14,000 feet—but only one that offers you four different ways of reaching the summit. A car, a bus, a cog railroad, a strong pair of legs—they'll all get you to the top of Pike's Peak.

However you get there, remember you'll be dealing with high altitudes. The air is much thinner and much cooler. For every 1000 feet you rise in altitude, plan on a 4-degree temperature drop. You can also plan on an absolutely awe-inspiring view.

The view from the summit stretches more than 165 miles eastward towards Kansas. This very view inspired Katherine Lee Bates to compose "America the Beautiful" in 1893.

For more information on any of the Colorado sites, contact the Colorado Tourism Board, 5500 South Syracuse Circle No. 267, Englewood, Colorado, 80111, (303) 779-1067.

Connecticut

Wadsworth Atheneum

The nation's first free art museum, the Wadsworth Atheneum in Hartford is nationally recognized for its fine collection. The museum contains more than 40,000 works which include paintings and sculptures from all major periods. Museum galleries also include rooms of period furniture, glass, textiles, and silver. The Lions Gallery of the Senses is a very special aspect of the museum as it features exhibits tailored to the visually handicapped.

This big little museum is open Tuesday through Sunday, with admission on Thursday being free. It is located at 600 Main Street, Hartford, Connecticut, 06103. To call just dial (203) 278-2670.

Mystic Marinelife Aquarium and Seaport Museum

The historic harbor town of Mystic sports two marine-life attractions, the aquarium and museum. The Mystic Marinelife Aquarium contains over 2000 living specimens in its 34 different exhibits. The "living" museum recreates a 19th century maritime village—complete with period ships, buildings and shops.

The Marine Theater in the Aquarium stars dophins, sea lions and whales in its hourly shows. Outdoors, the Seal Island exhibit recreates the natural environment of seals and sea lions all year long. The Aquarium is located on Coogan Boulevard. The telephone number is (203) 536-3323.

Just a bit down the road on Route 27, one can find the Mystic Seaport Museum. Artisans demonstrate different crafts like boat building or sail making throughout the day. The museum has its own planetarium, too. The last of the wooden whaling ships, the Charles W. Morgan, is another prize of the museum. The museum is open all year, although steam ship rides are available May through October only. The telephone number is (203) 572-0711.

Yale University

The architecture of the Yale campus provides examples of some of the finest Gothic buildings in the States. Take a guided walking tour of the university that includes Connecticut Hall where Nathan Hale and Noah Webster studied. Tours meet hourly at Phelps Gate, off College Street at the historic New Haven green.

Your tour may also include a walk through the Beinecke Rare Book Library that houses a Gutenberg bible, original Audubon prints, and medieval manuscripts, among other treasures. The building itself is noteworthy because it is windowless; however, translucent marble slabs allow a pinkish light to color the inner space.

Yale also has two superb art museums. The Yale University Art Gallery is the oldest college art museum in America and has outstanding American decorative art dating from 1700. Its collection also includes Pre-Columbian, Oriental, African, Italian Renaissance, and 20th century art works. Across the street, the Yale Center for British Art contains only British art—paintings, drawings, rare books, and sculpture. Both museums are on Chapel Street.

For information on the Yale tours, call (203) 436-8330. Beinecke's phone number is (203) 436-8438. You can reach the Yale University Art Gallery at (203) 436-0574. And the phone number of the Center for British Art is (203) 436-3909. All museums are free.

Delaware

Rehoboth Beach
Rehoboth Beach, on Delaware's Atlantic Coast in Sussex County, is an extremely popular summer resort. The swimming is terrific, as is the sailing, surfing, and sailboating. Oriented towards families, the area prides itself on being free of crass commercialism. A boardwalk with shops, restaurants, and amusement attractions adds summer atmosphere—enhanced by the serious volleyball games happening on the beach nearby.

Surf and deep sea fishing are excellent in the Rehoboth bay area—as are clamming and crabbing (though you've got to know the right spots). As wonderful a summer resort as Rehoboth is, why not try the beaches in the off-season? The crowds aren't there, and the prices aren't either. There's something serene about strolling the beach when no one else is there.

For more information, you can contact the Rehoboth Chamber of Commerce, 73 Rehoboth Avenue, Box 216, Rehoboth Beach, Delaware 19971-0216, (800) 441-1329.

Winterthur
Winterthur Museum and Gardens holds a superb collection of American decorative arts—more than 70,000 authentic objects that reflect styles from 1650 to 1850. Winterthur, the 200

room country estate of H.F. du Pont, houses his extraordinary collection in a nine-story building on 200 beautifully landscaped acres.

The quality of pieces at Winterthur are well-displayed in authentic settings. Du Pont imported such backdrops as a parlor from Pennsylvania, a drawing room from Virginia, and a 17th-century room from Massachusetts.

The museum offers a variety of guided tours with special spring and Christmas tours available by reservation. Winterthur is located on Route 52, six miles northwest of Wilmington. For tour information and reservations, call (302) 654-1548.

Halgey Museum

On the site of the original du Pont Company's black powder mills along the Brandywine River, the Hagley Museum gives you a taste of 19th century industry and home life.

The main exhibit building shows America's growth from water powered mills to electric powered industry. In the Powder Yards, water still powers a waterwheel, turbine, and hydroelectric plant. Further upstream is Eleutherian Mills, the original du Pont home, furnished with the artifacts of 5 generations of du Ponts. A barn filled with carriages and wagons, offices and workshops, and beautifully landscaped gardens offer further glimpses of the life of a millowner in the 19th century.

For more information, you can write The Hagley Museum, Box 3630, Wilmington, Delaware, 19807, (302) 658-2400.

Florida

The Ringling Museums

John Ringling (of the Circus fame) willed his dream palace, C'ad'zan, to the state of Florida. The 30 room opulent mansion, on 68 landscaped acres, is part of the greater Ringling Museum complex which also includes the Museum of the Circus, the John and Mabel Ringling Museum of Art, and the Asolo, America's only original 18th century Italian theater.

The Ringling Museum of Art contains an impressive collection of Baroque works. There, you can see the most complete grouping from Ruben's "Triumph of the Eucharist" series. 20th century art is exhibited in the Contemporary Gallery.

The Museum of the Circus shows off memorabilia collected from the "Greatest Show on Earth." While the emphasis is on the Ringling Brothers Circus, the museum has other historical exhibits dating back to the Roman Circus.

Ringling imported from Asolo, Italy, a theater that was built for Queen Catherine Cornaro of Cyprus in 1798. He reconstructed it. Today, it is an operating theater and opera house on the grounds of the complex.

The Ringling Museums are located on US 41, 3 miles north of Sarasota. For schedules, call (813) 355-5101.

St. Augustine City

Known as the oldest city in the U.S., San Augustin Antiguo (old St. Augustine) has preserved its 16th century feel. Walking the narrow streets, you can view many historic homes and buildings. Authentically costumed people complete the ancient scene.

You must stop at the Fountain of Youth, which celebrates the site of Ponce De Leon's first search for a potion of eternal youth. From there, you can walk to the Lightner Museum which features an extensive collection of antiques and mechanical musical instruments.

Two Spanish fortresses, the Castillo de San Marcos National Monument and Fort Matanzas, offer another aspect of Florida's past. The Oldest House on St. Francis Street has Spanish, British, and American influences.

For more information on Old St. Augustine, write the Chamber of Commerce at 10 Castillo Dr., St. Augustine, Florida, 32084.

Disneyworld

In 1967, Disney transformed 28,000 acres of Orlando, Florida swampland into Disneyworld, the world's largest tourist attraction. The acres surrounding Disneyworld have been set aside as a wildlife refuge.

You should plan on two days to experience all of the Magic Kingdom. Another two days are needed to properly view the wonders of EPCOT (Experimental Prototype Community of Tomorrow). Metro liners let you ride through the time of the dinosaurs to the world of the future. Underneath the Magic Kingdom lie 1 1/2 miles of tunnels, where most of the special effects are controlled. To see parts of this "Backstage Magic," you must arrange a tour in advance.

Disneyworld is really a complete village with restaurants, campgrounds, golf courses, and hotels. For more information, write Disneyworld in Orlando, Florida.

Georgia

Cherry Blossom Festival

Mid-March marks Macon's 10-day celebration of the cherry blossom and the arrival of Spring. More than 100,000 Yoshino cherry trees line Macon's streets—coloring the air with their beautiful blossoms and fragrance.

All sorts of activities occur during the festival, the highlight of which is the spectacular Cherry Blossom Parade. Musical events are always going on—be it dixieland, marching band, bluegrass, or symphony.

Macon is duly proud of its southern history and hospitality. The city has many fine examples of antebellum estates, and the restored downtown offers many reminders of Macon's past.

For more information, contact the Cherry Blossom Festival, Southern Trust Building, Suite 1110, 682 Cherry Street, Macon, Georgia, 31201.

Stone Mountain Park

Stone Mountain Park is 3200 acres of entertainment, recreation, and education for the entire family. Activities include camping, ice skating, laser shows, historical building tours, and antique auto and music museums.

The Park also commemorates the Confederacy with a 90 x 190 foot carving of Confederate President Jefferson Davis, General Robert E. Lee, and General Stonewall Jackson on an exposed granite mountain wall. Cable cars give visitors a close-up view of the tribute.

Boating and fishing are available on Stone Mountain Lake, as are waterslides and sandy beaches. The golf course, situated so as to provide a superb view of the mountain and carving, is also rated among the top 25 in the country.

Stone Mountain Park is open year round. For more information on what the park offers, contact Georgia's Stone Mountain Park, P.O. Box 778, Stone Mountain, Georgia, 30086, (404) 498-5600.

Six Flags Over Georgia

The quintessential family theme park, Six Flags Over Georgia in Atlanta, offers shows, attractions, rides, and activities to satisfy everyone's idea of family fun. Kids will get a kick out of the Looney Tunes characters parading around the park, and adults will enjoy the big-name entertainment performing at night. There's even a rock club for teens called Graffiti.

Thrills abound aboard a Six Flags roller coaster ride. If your appetite for excitement is still not sated, you must see the new High Diving Show, the conclusion of which involves a spectacular fire dive.

The park is open daily during the summer and on weekends in May, September, October and November. The park is located in Atlanta, off I-285. For more information, contact the Georgia Department of Industry and Trade, 230 Peachtree Street, NW, Atlanta, Georgia, 30303, (404) 656-3593.

Hawaii

Diamond Head and Waikiki

Diamond Head, an extinct volcano, is located on the southernmost tip of the island of Oahu. Hawaiian legend says it was once the home of Pele, the Fire Goddess. Overlooking the resort beach of Waikiki, it is home to a slightly different clientele today.

Surfing is tops at Waikiki for both the beginner and the expert. Catamaran riding and outrigger canoeing are also popular activities. Regattas and races are scheduled regularly. Waikiki also offers easy access to charter fishing boats, golf courses, and tennis courts.

Both orchestral and choral concerts in the Waikiki Shell offer pearls of culture in a beautiful outdoor setting.

For more information, you can contact the information office, Waikiki Beach Resort, 2270 Kalakaua Ave., Honolulu, Hawaii, 96815.

Haleakala National Park

Maui's most thrilling spectacle is Mt. Haleakala, the volcano with a crater of 25 square miles which is large enough to hold Manhattan captive. Polynesian legend claims that the god Maui captured the sun and kept it in the volcanic crater in order to give his people more daylight hours.

The drop from rim to floor is 3000 feet. Hiking

and horse trails wind down the crater to its moonlike surface, where National Parks rangers maintain several cabins. Scientists have set up research centers on Haleakala's rim to study the sun and constellations. Dubbed "Science City," the centers include astronomical Observatories and Satellite Tracking Stations.

More information can be obtained from the Hawaii Visitor's Bureau, 2270 Kalakau Avenue, Honolulu, Hawaii, 96815.

St. Benedict's and Star of the Sea

The big island of Hawaii is the site of two churches with brilliantly painted murals.

St. Benedict's at Honaunau is the oldest Catholic church on the island. Built in 1875, the church is known for its exquisitely colorful murals. Biblical scenes illustrate the inner sanctuary of the church. The murals decorating the walls in the Star of the Sea Catholic church in Kalapana are equally inspiring. Not as old as those at St. Benedict's, the murals at Star of the Sea were painted by a priest about 50 years ago.

For more information, you can contact the Hawaii Visitor's Bureau, 2270 Kalakau Avenue, Honolulu, Hawaii, 96815.

IDAHO

Sun Valley

A world-class winter ski resort, Sun Valley has few rivals for its Rocky Mountain powder. With 58 miles of trails, there's no chance of running out of runs. The mountain is oriented so that it's possible to catch the sun on most slopes, too.

World Cup races are often held at Sun Valley, and there are races for recreational skiers too. Helicopter skiing is available if you want to ski back country powder. Nordic terrain is also accessible—either by bus or by helicopter.

As varied as the skiing opportunities at Sun Valley in winter, summer also offers many different recreational activities. Two challenging 18 hole golf courses and more than 100 tennis courts have the Rocky Mountains as a backdrop. Both games take on a different tenor in such a setting.

Horse back riding is also popular because of the trails winding through Sun Valley and the Sawtooth Mountains. Sun Valley has several outdoor heated pools and outdoor ice-skating rinks for budding Dorothy Hamills. Hang-gliding and fishing round out the activities.

For more information, call (800) 635-8261.

National Old-time Fiddler's Contest

The third week in June is the time for old-time fiddlers to rosin up their bows in preparation for the National Old-time Fiddler's Contest in Weiser. The contest serves both as an appreciation of the fiddling art and a preservation of the fiddle's musical heritage.

The Contest has a variety of divisions for men and women and juniors and seniors. Most winners receive a cash prize and trophy. Since each contestant must play 4 minutes of music including hoedowns and waltzes, listeners are treated to some pretty fine fiddling.

The contest also features exhibits which display the history and artifacts of old-time fiddling. Some of the fiddlers play dressed in old-time garb, every detail intact including whiskers.

For more information (for players and listeners), write the National Old-time Fiddler's Contest, Chamber of Commerce, 8 East Idaho, Weiser, Idaho, 83672.

White Water Rafting

The ultimate adventure may very well be a white water rafting trip down an Idaho river—the Snake, the Middlefork, the Selway, or the legendary "River of No Return" deemed unnavigable when first observed by Lewis and Clark.

A white water rafting trip enables you to experience all facets of the West's outdoors—riding through crashing waves, resting on hot beaches, floating through deep canyon gorges, and sleeping beneath crystalline stars.

There are a variety of white water tours available. The Idaho Travel Council publishes a booklet entitled "Summer and Fall Vacation Package Directory" that lists many of the organizations offering such trips. The address is Statehouse, Boise, Idaho, 83720, (800) 635-7820.

Illinois

The Sears Tower

At 1454 feet, the Sears Building is the tallest building in the World. From the skydeck, you have an extraordinary view of the city. You'll see the Loop which circles an 8 block square and is the business and political heart of the city. You'll also see the Magnificent Mile, a stretch of Michigan Avenue flanked by very cosmospolitan stores and boutiques. And of course, there is Lake Shore Drive and Lake Michigan, bordering the city on the east.

The Sears Tower is located at Wacker Drive and Jackson Boulevard. You can enter the skydeck from 9 a.m. to midnight, seven days a week. There is an admission fee.

If you need more information, you can call (312) 875-9696.

Abraham Lincoln's Hometown

There are many sights associated with Lincoln in Springfield, the town in which he lived before moving to Washington, D.C. If you're looking for a walking tour, follow the Lincoln Post Road, the route Lincoln took as a postal clerk. The old State Capitol is where Lincoln gave his "House Divided" speech.

Tours are available through Lincoln's house and the place where he practiced law. You can see the Lincoln Family Pew at the First Presbyterian Church or the Lincoln Ledger, a record of Lincoln's accounts, at Springfield Marine Bank. You can also pay your respects to Lincoln. The granite spire of his tomb rises 117 feet above the cemetary. Civil War statuary bedecks the top of the tomb's terrace.

Get a Mr. Lincoln's Hometown Kit from the Convention and Visitor's Bureau, 624 East Adams Street, Springfield, Illinois, 62701, (217) 789-2360.

Shawnee National Forest

The Shawnee consists of 260,000 acres of forest, rolling through the hills and valleys of southern Illinois. Hiking, fishing, boating and ballooning are just some of the ways to experience the forest.

The natural wonders are fantastic—trails, springs, canyons, even rock formations more than 200 million years old. The forest is also a sanctuary for wildlife. In fact, parts of some roads are closed so as not to disturb the birds. Most of the roads, however, are open year-round.

A dozen different towns offer entrance to the forest. To find out more about the park, contact the Forest Supervisor, Shawnee National Forest, USDA-Forest Service, Highway 45 South, Harrisburg, Illinois, 62946, (618) 253-7114.

Indiana

Covered Bridge Festival

Laying claim to the largest number of covered bridges of any county in the nation, Parke County hosts an annual covered bridge fest beginning the second Friday in October. Along with highlighting the bridges, the festival also features local crafts, baked goods and entertainment.

Rockville is the center of the celebration, with a craft fair on the town square. At historic Billie Creek Village, visitors can talk with residents dressed in 19th century costumes and concerned with the issues of that period.

As you tour the 34 different covered bridges, you can visit many villages enroute—each with its own special charm and delights. The festival is also one of the best ways to enjoy the autumnal hues of Indiana.

For more information, contact Parke County Inc., Box 165, Rockville, Indiana, 47872-0165, (317) 569-5226.

The Johnny Appleseed Festival

For two days at the end of September, at the peak of apple picking time, Fort Wayne celebrates John Chapman, a.k.a. Johnny Appleseed. Its Pioneer Village returns the visitor to the sensory pleasures of the 1800's. And the Antiques and Collectibles Flea Market offers old-time relics of this era.

You'll get a feel for pioneer country Indiana through the continuous entertainment that the Festival provides. A Fife and Drum Corps shares the stage with bluegrass musicians. Square dancing, puppet shows, and the Dulcimer society add to the merriment. A Drill and Weapon show rounds out the mix.

For more information, contact Fort Wayne Parks and Recreation, 705 E. State, Fort Wayne, Indiana, 46805, (219) 427-1270.

Circus City Festival

Did you know that Peru, Indiana, was the permanent home of many of the travelling circuses during the nineteenth and early twentieth centuries? The Circus City Festival, occurring in July, is a celebration of that heritage.

Since many of the townsfolk remain rooted in circus life, the acts include flying trapeze, high wire, perch pole, unicycle, balancing acts, and—of course—clowns. And the costumes are spectacular. The Festival also provides a scholarship fund to help young performers who are seeking a college education.

A street parade and amusement rides combine with crafts and foods to make this a real carnival atmosphere. For more information, contact the Circus City Festival Office, Broadway and 7th, Peru, Indiana, 46970, (317) 472-3981.

IOWA

Amana Colonies

These seven German villages date back to 1844, when a group of Europeans settled in the area to escape religious persecution. They primarily framed the 26,000 acres of land and also built homes, churches, mills and shops—all of which you can visit today.

You are free to walk around the villages and look at the distinctive architectural styles. There are also several museums. You can tour the woolen mills, furniture shops and meat shops, as well.

Amana has several wineries that make unusual wines. Piestengel (rhubarb) and dandelion wine are two specialties. The area is also known for its down-home German cooking. The villages are charming in any season, although a visit between July and August affords a vision of nearby Lily Lake blossoming with lotus lilies.

For more information, you can contact the Amana Colonies Travel Council, Amana, Iowa, 52203, (319) 622-3828.

Terrace Hill

Terrace Hill, the official residence of Iowa's governor, is a magnificent Midwestern palace, recognized as one of the finest examples of Second Empire-style architecture in the States. Built in 1870 for a local banker and businessman, the house was designed by the architect of the Chicago Water tower.

Most of the house has been restored to reflect the Victorian elegance of its time. Mahogany-framed mirrors, crystal chandeliers, and laminated rosewood parlor furniture all date from the civil war period. Hallway stencil designs are reproductions of patterns popular during the 1890's. A magnificent large stained-glass window greets visitors reaching the landing of the grand staircase.

The main floor rooms are open to the public, March through December. The second floor contains the governor's private offices and guest suite. The third floor used to be the servant's quarters but is now the private living area for the governor's family.

Terrace Hill is located at 2300 Grand Avenue, Des Moines, Iowa, 50312, (515) 281-3604.

Mississippi Belle/Spirit of Dubuque

What better way to experience the mighty Mississippi River than a paddlewheeler cruise? The Mississippi Belle and Spirit of Dubuque both offer 1-1/2 hour sightseeing trips. The Mississippi Belle also offers a daylong cruise that travels 100 miles down the Mississippi.

Spring, summer, or fall, you can enjoy the gorgeous scenery that is only enhanced by a swing band's tunes of yesteryear. The Mississippi Belle is a triple-deck paddlewheeler with room enough for 800 passengers. The Spirit of Dubuque is a double-deck paddlewheeler, holding 377 passengers. Reservations are required for each.

For reservations or schedules, contact Robert River Rides, 62 Locust Street, Dubuque, Iowa, 52001, (319) 583-5379 or 1761.

Kansas

Little House on the Prairie

Near Independence, Little House on the Prairie recreates the log cabin on the site where Laura Ingalls Wilder, the author of the Little House on the Prairie books, grew up. The Ingalls family lived there in a one-room cabin in the 1870's.

The cabin, a one-room country schoolhouse, and an early rural post office represent the world of Laura Ingalls Wilder, a world which has also been popularized in the television show "Little House on the Prairie."

The buildings are open for viewing from May 15 to September 1. Little House on the Prairie is located at Southwest US-75, Independence, Kansas, 67301, (316) 331-1890.

International Pancake Race

Every Shrove Tuesday (the day before Ash Wednesday) the women of Liberal don housedresses, aprons, and head scarves to compete in the annual International Pancake Race.

According to legend, more than 500 years ago, a woman was using up cooking fats (forbidden on Lent) by making pancakes. Hearing the bell toll the shriving service, she quickly ran to the church—apron still on and skillet in hand. The next year, all her neighbors carried their skillets to church.

The race was originally run in Olney, England

(and is still run there, as a matter of fact). Liberal started its race in 1950. Dressed in proper uniform and carrying skillets, women run the S-shaped course, flipping their pancakes twice.

For more information, contact the Convention and Tourism Bureau, Box 1626, Liberal, Kansas, 67901, (316) 624-9425.

Eisenhower Center

The Eisenhower Center includes the Eisenhower Family Home, The Museum and Library, and the Place of Meditation where both Dwight and Mamie Eisenhower are buried. The museum has many exhibits on Eisenhower's time in the military and on his presidency.

The library houses his administration's papers and is available for scholary research. The family home still contains its original furnishings. You can also visit the Visitor's Center and see a free movie about Eisenhower's life.

The buildings are open year round from 9-5 and are located at Southeast Fourth Street, Abilene, Kansas, 67410, (913) 263-4751.

Kentucky

Kentucky Derby/Churchill Downs

"Unless you go to Kentucky and with your own eyes behold the Kentucky Derby, you ain't never been nowhere and you ain't never seen nothin'." So said an old Kentuckian, referring to Kentucky's ultimate experience. The Derby is always held the first Saturday in May, although the Kentucky Derby Festival starts 10 days before.

The most prestigious thoroughbred horse race in America, the Derby is for 3-year-olds only and is run on a 1-1/4 mile track at Churchill Downs where the first Derby was run in 1875. The Grandstand and Club seat more than 45,000.

There is also a Kentucky Derby museum at Churchill Downs in Louisville that features multimedia presentations and exhibits on the Derby. The Museum is located at Churchill Downs, 704 Central Avenue, Gate 1, (502) 637-1111. For general information on Churchill Downs, call (502) 636-3541.

Fort Knox

Though known primarily for the Gold Depository on its land, Fort Knox is actually a large U.S. Military Reservation, spreading 109,362 acres. It was named for the Revolutionary War General Henry Knox.

There is a Patton Museum of Cavalry and Armor on the grounds in Keyes Park. The museum has exhibits featuring armor from the Revolutionary War to the War in Vietnam. Most of Patton's personal effects are on display as well. There is also a substantial amount of armor that was captured by Patton's troops during World War II.

The Gold Depository is a 2 story granite, steel and concrete bullion depository containing most of the U.S. gold reserve. The combination of the lock is divided up between staff members so that no one knows the complete pattern. Tourists can look at the building from the road.

Fort Knox is located on US 31 W and US 60, south of Louisville. The Patton Museum is off US 31 W in Keyes Park. The Gold Depository is on Gold Vault Road.

Cumberland Falls State Park

Cumberland Falls is also known as the "Niagara of the South" because of the water's thunderous 68 foot drop. Under a full moon, the Falls show the only moonbow in the Western hemisphere.

There are many opportunities for hiking—11 miles of trail in the Daniel Boone Forest and 15 miles of trail inside the park. Fishing in the Cumberland River is also excellent. The river beneath the Falls offers scenic and challenging runs for rafters, canoers, and kayakers. Organized trips are operated by Cumberland Outdoor Adventure. Call them at (606) 523-0629 for more information.

The park is open from April through October and has sites for both tents and housekeeping cottages. For more information, contact Cumberland Falls State Park, Corbin, Kentucky, 40701, (606) 528-4121.

Louisiana

Oak Alley Plantation

Oak Alley Plantation was built by a French sugar planter in the late 1830's. He named it Oak Alley because of the 2 stately rows of oak trees stretching from the mansion to the Mississippi River.

Spared during the Civil War, Oak Alley had a series of owners before being purchased by Andrew Stewart in 1925. The plantation then became the first of the Great River Road plantations to be fully restored. Today, the decor of Oak Alley is just the same as it was when the Stewarts owned it. Many of the tour guides once worked for the Stewarts and know the house very well.

The mansion is open all year round. For more information, contact the Oak Alley Foundation, Rt. 2, Box 10, Vacherie, Louisiana, 70090, (504) 265-2151.

Delta Queen

The Delta Queen is one of the few remaining authentic riverboats—an original steamboat paddling her passengers down a great American river. Riding the Delta Queen brings you into a royal shipping world of teak handrails, Tiffany stained-glass windows, brass fittings, and an opulent mahogany Grand Staircase. Of course, the Delta Queen is listed on the National Register of Historic Places.

The Delta Queen offers many different cruise itineraries of varying lengths and routes. Each month also offers a different theme such as Big Bands in February and Fall Foliage in October. Sights on the Mississippi include some of Louisiana's magnificent mansions and classic plantations, as well as the Old State Capitol building in Baton Rouge.

For more information you can contact the Delta Queen at her Home Port Office, 511 Main Street, Cincinnati, Ohio, 45202, (800) 543-1949. Cruises begin in New Orleans, however.

Superdome

The Louisiana Superdome dominates the skyline of downtown New Orleans and has been the site of several of the last decade's Super Bowls. Less than a mile from the French Quarter, the building opened in 1975.

The ceiling is 273 feet high and the diameter of the dome is 680 feet. Here's a great piece of sports trivia for you: how many light fixtures does the Superdome have? 15,200. Superdome AstroTurf is affectionately called "Mardi Grass."

The Superdome is the home of the New Orleans Saints of the NFL, the Sugar Bowl and Tulane football. Tours are given daily except during certain sporting events. For rates and tour information, call (504) 587-3810.

Maine

Acadia National Park

Lucky for us, the U.S. government set aside twenty-two square miles on Mount Desert Island and created Acadia National Park. The island can trace its geologic beginnings back to the Ice Age when the glaciers left islands and inlets where once had been mountains.

The Park is open year-round. Trails that during the summer are peopled by hikers, horseback riders, and bikers turn over to cross-country skiers when the first snows come. There is a hard-surface road that will take you to the top of Cadillac Mountain. At 1530 feet, it is the highest point on the East Coast. The views offer a choice of mountains, islands, ocean or the interior.

From mid-June to early October, there are scheduled nature activities that may include walks, hikes, boat cruises, and evening programs. You can get information from the Visitor's Center upon arrival.

For more information on the park, contact Acadia National Park, P.O. Box 177, Bar Harbor, Maine, 04609, (207) 288-3338.

Lumberman's Museum

Lumbering has long been the foundation of Maine's economy—with coastal forests still covering more than 85 percent of the state. The

Lumberman's Museum pays homage to the Maine woodsman and his life over the past 150 or so years.

Nine buildings display more than 3000 artifacts including carpenter's tools, horse-drawn logging sleds, tractors, and even an early pulp truck. The evolution of the logging camp is suggested through a series of dioramas depicting life in the various camps.

Visitors should note the detail in a replica of a logging camp of the early 1800's. A cedar split-and-pole roof tops a building in which no nails were used in construction—adhering to the construction fashion of the time.

The museum is only open during the summer. For more information, contact the Patten Lumberman's Museum, Route 159, Patten, Maine, 04765, (207) 528-2650.

L.L. Bean Store
No piece of direct mail better conjures up Maine than an L.L. Bean catalog in your box. So visit the real thing—the L.L. Bean store in Freeport. L.L. Bean specializes in quality sportswear and sporting goods from snow shoes to sailboats. The store sells most of the items in the catalog at retail prices; however, you can get some real bargains at the L.L. Bean outlet department.

The sucess (and fame) of the L.L. Bean store has spurred the development of Freeport as a retail and outlet mecca. The city takes pride in its many distinctive shops and fine restaurants. Shoppers can also take advantage of such stores as the Anne Klein outlet, the Bass Shoe Factory outlet, the Dansk Factory outlet, and the Hathaway Shirt Factory outlet—to name just a few choice shops.

The hours for all shops vary. If you have a specific store in mind, your best bet is to call the shop to find out when it's open for business.

Maryland

Historic St. Mary's City

This outdoor history museum resides on the site of Maryland's first settlement and 17th century capital. The whole area is a testament to Maryland's early history. 66 acres of woodland, marsh, beach and bluffs have been set aside as the Chancellor's Point Natural History Area.

In the summer months, there are live presentations about the history of the area. The Godiah Spray Tobacco Plantation is a working reconstruction of a 17th century tobacco farm. You can walk around the buildings, viewing the tobacco barns, crops and farmhouses. A replica of Maryland's first state house contains exhibits on Maryland's history.

St. Mary's City also houses a replica of the Maryland Dove which was one of the first ships to sail to Maryland. You must have dinner in the model of a 17th century inn.

The area is located off Rt. 5 in St. Mary's City. For more information on any of the attractions, call (301) 862-1666 or 1634.

Assateague State and National Seashore Parks

Just south of the resort life of Ocean Beach lies the wild haunting beauty of Assateague Island. A 35-mile-long strip of land, Assateague Island has many places to explore among its windswept dunes and wildlife.

While the barrier island offers a great variety of wildlife, it is famous for the wild ponies that roam freely over the land. Visitors can also swim in the Atlantic, off the coast of Assateague. There are also many nature trails that take you into the heart of the island.

You can visit the island from sunrise to sunset. It is located on Route 611 at the Atlantic Ocean. The telephone number is (301) 641-2120 or 1441.

Antietam National Battlefield

This civil war battleground marks the spot of the bloodiest single day of battle in American history. One pauses at Antietam, thinking back on those days when brother fought brother at the line where north met south.

Most men fell along Bloody Lane. You can also see such historical landmarks as the Burnside Bridge and Drunkard Church. To visit all these sights, pick up a self-guided driving tour brochure from the information desk.

Antietam is located on Route 65 in Sharpsburg and open all year long. The telephone number is (301) 432-5124.

Massachusetts

Plimoth Plantation

One might say that American history begins at Plimoth Plantation, featuring, as it does, a full-scale replica of the Mayflower II, the 1627 Pilgrim Village, and a Wampanoag Indian Campsite.

Not only are the physical exhibits as historically accurate as possible, but so too are the museum staff attending them. Staff people are specially trained. They dress in period clothing, speak in the dialects of the time, and live the routine of the colonial farming community. Visitors may talk to these "colonists" and learn why they left England and how they are faring in their new land.

A hands-on museum, Plimoth Plantation encourages its visitors to try such activities as grinding corn and riving clapboard. You may even spend a little time in the stocks if you're not careful.

Located in Plymouth, Plimoth Plantation is open mid-March through November. For more information, contact Plimoth Plantation, P.O. Box 1620, Plymouth, Massachusetts, 02360, (617) 746-1622.

Tanglewood

The summer home of the internationally famous Boston Symphony Orchestra, Tanglewood provides a beautiful Berkshire background for both classical and popular artists. In addition to the regular concerts of the BSO, one can hear chamber music concerts and contemporary singers. The Boston Pops makes an annual appearance, as well.

What makes a concert at Tanglewood so special is the locale. Set on more than 400 acres, Tanglewood is in Lenox, right in the heart of the Berkshire countryside. One can hear concerts in the covered music pavillion, casually known as "the Shed." Or one can pack a picnic and sit out on the lawn to hear the concert.

Saturday mornings are open rehearsals when the Symphony practices the evening's performance. Tickets are reduced, and you can sit in the Shed or on the lawn. Seiji Ozawa serves as artistic director. Other well-known guest conductors also appear.

For more information on Tanglewood, you can contact the Boston Symphony Orchestra, Symphony Hall, Boston, Massachusetts, 02115, (617) 266-1492.

Faneuil Hall

The Faneuil Hall Marketplace is a terrific testament of urban renewal and the renaissance of the city. A renovated marketsquare in downtown Boston, Fanueil Hall consists of three huge halls: Quincy Market, North Market, and South Market.

Quincy Market, the central building, offers a smorgasbord of food choices. Chances are, whatever it is you're craving will be available in abundance. Both the North and South Market buildings are filled with extremely interesting specialty shops whose goods come from all over the world. The variety of wares makes both browsing and buying enjoyable activities.

The Boston Fine Arts Museum has opened a branch on the fifth floor of South Market, so you can even sneak a bit of culture between purchases. Dancers, singers, musicians, and jugglers entertain outdoors during the summer months, delighting all.

For more information on the Faneuil Hall Marketplace, contact the Boston visitor info/line, (617) 267-6446.

Michigan

Henry Ford Museum/Greenville Village

At Greenville Village, you can visit the homes and workplaces of famous and non-famous Americans. In so doing, you'll experience the changing ideas and ways of life between 1800 and 1950.

Village attractions include Thomas Edison's laboratory where he devised the lightbulb among other inventions and Noah Webster's home where he created the dictionary. You can also visit Orville and Wilbur Wright's home and cycle shop where they designed the airplane. Henry Ford's birthplace and the Ohio farmstead of industrialist Harvey Firestone are also open for visitors.

The Henry Ford Museum is really a celebration of pop culture Americana from the turn of the century to the 1950's. Past exhibits have included "Streamlining America" which featured products with efficient and aesthetic designs and "Yesterday's Tomorrows," different visions of the world of the future.

The Henry Ford Museum also sponsors a series of "Great Escape" weekends which celebrate the popular music, fashions, politics, and entertainment of various decades. The Museum has a theater that revives popular plays of the early century, too.

Greenville Village and Henry Ford Museum are

open year-round. Depending on the season, you can ride in horse-drawn carriages, sleighs, antique cars, steam trains, or a paddlewheel river boat.

The Henry Ford Museum and Greenville Village are located in Dearborn, Michigan, 48121, (800) 835-2246.

Mackinac Island

If you're interested in Indian culture, military life, or the War of 1812, a stop-over on Mackinac Island is a must. Fort Mackinac, on a bluff overlooking the water, survived both British and American occupation during the War of 1812. Costumed guides give tours of the fort and its war memorabilia.

The island also has hourly musket demonstrations and cannon firings. Tours are available through historical houses such as the Biddle House and the Beaumont Memorial. An old Indian Dormitory provides an interesting lesson in Indian life. The sandy beaches by the Water Gate make for a nice afternoon respite.

Mackinac Island is located right near Mackinaw City. For more information, write Mackinac Island State Park Commission, Box 3002Bl, Lansing, Michigan, 48909. The winter telephone number is (517) 322-1319, and the summer number is (906) 847-3328.

Tulip Time Festival

A festival celebrating flowers and Holland's Dutch heritage, Tulip Time dates back to 1929 when the city first planted its colorful bulbs. Today, the Tulip Festival is the third largest festival in the United States. Tulips blossom every where—in front of houses, businesses and down the eight miles of Tulip Lanes.

Tulip Time also features special parades and Dutch dances. The dancers dress in authentic costumes, down to the wooden klompen that they wear on their feet. Barbershop quartets add their harmony to the festival.

If you attend the festival, you must visit Windmill Island where a 200-year-old Dutch windmill is flanked by 100,000 tulips. One can also visit "Little Netherlands," a miniature Dutch village nearby.

The festival occurs in May in Holland, Michigan. The Tulip Time General Information Center can be found at 8th and Pine Avenue. Call them at (616) 396-4221 for information about Tulip Time.

Minnesota

Itasca State Park/Great River Road

With 32,000 acres of gorgeous trees, Itasca is the source of the Mississippi River. The Mississippi River begins its journey to the Gulf of Mexico and so, too, does an extraordinary scenic drive, the Great River Road. Beginning as a trickling stream, the river is crossable upon a path of stepping stones. It then winds through the metro areas of Minneapolis and St. Paul to its widest point in Minnesota, Lake Pepin. It continues to flow downward through more river towns in southeastern Minnesota.

People have spied as many as 149 species of birds in one season at Itasca. To view wildlife (as well as imposing trees), you should plan to visit the Precher's Grove. Your visit must also include Peace Pipe Vista, an overlook that offers a spectacular view of the area.

For more information, contact the Minnesota Office of Tourism, 240 Bremer Building, 419 North Robert Street, St. Paul, Minnesota, 55101.

Winter Carnival

America's premier winter festival is the Winter Carnival in Saint Paul with its parades, pageantry, skiing, and ice skating events. The two grand attractions of the Carnival are the elegant ice palace and the re-enactment of the Legend of Winter Carnival.

The Ice Palace is made of 50,000 blocks of ice, rising 15 stories above the ground. Winter activities include figure skating, curling, cross-country skiing, sleigh rides and band concerts. There is also a special winter playground for children—with snow and ice sculptures to slide down and climb on.

Another highlight of the Carnival is the 200 team softball competition. The hitch is that the game is played on the slippery ice of McCarron's lake.

For more information, contact the St. Paul Convention & Tourism Commission, Landmark Center, B-100, St. Paul, Minnesota, 55102, (800) 328-8322, ext. 983.

Iron Range Resources—Hill Annex Mine Tour

The Hill Annex is one of the largest natural ore mines in the United States. One can ride to the bottom, looking at the huge mining equipment, conveyor system and loading pocket enroute. At the bottom of the mine, you can see deep into the underground mine shaft.

If you go to the top of the ore stockpile, you'll have a terrific view of the mine below and the beautiful scenery adjacent to the mine. The regular season runs from Memorial Day to the end of September. Special tours running through the end of October can be arranged by reservation.

If you want more information, you can write the Iron Range Resources—Hill Annex Mine Tour, P.O. Box 376, Columet, Minnesota, 55716, (218) 247-7215.

Mississippi

Jimmie Rodgers Museum

"The Father of Country Music," Jimmie Rodgers was born in Meridian, site of the Jimmie Rodgers Museum and Memorial Festival. The museum celebrates the life of Jimmie Rodgers, displaying family portraits, records and sheet music, letters and other personal effects.

The museum also has an interesting exhibit of railroad equipment from the steam engine era. Rodgers once worked on the railroad, picking up the nickname "The Singing Brakeman."

Rodgers was the first person to be inducted into the Country Music Hall of Fame in Nashville. During the fourth week of May, Meridian sponsors a country music festival where top country artists gather to pay homage to Rodgers's contributions to American music.

For more information, contact the Jimmie Rodgers Museum, P.O. Box 4555, West Station, Meridian, Mississippi, 39301, (601) 485-1808.

Gulf Coast

The Mississippi Gulf Coast stretches 26 miles. 26 miles of gorgeous beaches and beautiful sparkly water. 26 miles of fresh seafood like shrimp, crabs, oysters, red-snapper, flounder and sea trout.

If you're looking for history, you can tour the spectacular mansion of Grasslawn, built in 1836.

You can also visit Beauvoir, which was the last home of Jefferson Davis, the Confederacy's first and only president. Boats run to Ship Island, site of historic Fort Massachusetts. The Biloxi lighthouse on the Coast was built in 1848 and painted black to commemorate Lincoln's assassination.

There are 14 golf courses on the Mississippi Gulf Coast. And weather's generally not a problem, with a January average high being 68 degrees. There are plenty of fishing opportunities, too—drop your hook off a public pier or charter a fishing boat and go off to sea.

For more information on the Mississippi Gulf Coast, write the Harrison County Tourism Commission, P.O. Box 4554, Biloxi, Mississippi, 39531.

Natchez Trace

The Natchez Trace Parkway is a part of the National Park System, set up to preserve the original frontier road and its history. As you drive down the trace, you can stop to explore the many archaeological sites, landmarks and nature trails off the road.

You may find the remains of a house or an abandoned mine—reminders of the people who lived by or travelled this route. From 1880-1920, this road was the most active in the Old Southwest. Its travellers included boatsmen, soldiers, postmen, missionaries, Indians, and pioneers.

There are no overnight facilities along the parkway, although there are campsites. For a map of the Trace and its historical landmarks, write Rural Route 1, NT-143, Tupelo, Mississippi, 38801, (601) 842-1572.

Missouri

The Gateway Arch

America's tallest monument, the Gateway Arch is part of the Jefferson National Expansion Memorial. It pays tribute to Jefferson and other pioneers who pushed the boundaries of the country to the Pacific. Designed by Eero Saarinen, the Arch offers a 30-mile panoramic view.

To reach the top of the arch, you must first board a capsule train fifty feet below the ground. Each capsule holds five people and is designed so that you will always be in normal position throughout, even as your route curves upward. At the top, you will find yourself 630 feet above the ground—with an extaordinary view of St. Louis and the Illinois side of the Mississippi.

You can get to the top of the arch all year round. For more information or advance reservations, contact the Bi-state Development Agency, Arch Reservations, 707 North First Street, St. Louis, Missouri, 63102, (314) 982-1410.

Silver Dollar City

Silver Dollar City is a major theme park set in a 19th century village. In addition to the comedy, music and other entertainment peppered throughout the dwellings of the city, there are more than 30 resident craftsmen demonstrating their old-time skills.

Popular activities include splashing down the water slide, "American Plunge," and floating through the "Lost River of the Ozarks" on a six-passenger boat. Silver Dollar City also sponsors several exciting festivals featuring quilts, country music, and crafts. Broom making, basketweaving, candy making and dulcimer making are among the crafts demonstrated daily.

Silver Dollar City is open from the beginning of May to the end of October. The theme park is located in Ozark Mountain country in southwestern Missouri. For more information call (800) 641-4202.

Country Club Plaza

Country Club Plaza, in Kansas City, was America's first shopping center, developed in the 1920's. Today, it remains an elegant environment, offering shopping, dining and nightlife against a backdrop of fountains and Spanish architecture.

Within the 14 block district, Country Club Plaza contains more than 150 shops including Gucci, Macy's and Brooks Brothers. Gazing upon the plaza's ornate towers, statues and artwork, you can't help but notice the European influence.

At Thanksgiving, a celebration surrounds the lighting of the 52 miles of lights and the transformation of the Plaza into a fairy land. To find out more information about Country Club Plaza write the Convention and Visitors Bureau of Greater Kansas City, 1100 Main Street, Suite 2550, Kansas City, Missouri, 64105.

Montana

Glacier National Park

In the heart of the Montana Rockies, Glacier National Park contains about 50 glaciers and 200 lakes. The streams are crystal clear and offer wonderful opportunities for fishing. Exquisite wildflowers, thundering waterfalls, sheer cliffs and lush forests add to the park's crystallized beauty.

One can travel the trails on foot, horseback, or cross-country skis. All forms of locomotion will take you to the alpine meadows and mountain chalets. Granite Park Chalet and Sperry Chalet offer overnight accommodations. Glacier also hosts a population of grizzly bears and strongly protects their habitat.

The park is open year-round. A late autumn visit will let you see bald eagles feeding on spawning salmon in lower McDonald Creek. An early spring outing lets you see tiny colorful wildflowers pushing their way through the snow on the ground. A 50-mile east/west road goes across the Continental Divide and then cuts across the Garden Wall. It's a spectacular drive but not open in the winter.

For more information, contact the Superintendent, Glacier National Park, West Glacier, Montana, 59936.

Custer Battlefield National Monument

Southeast of Billings, there is a monument

that rests on the site of "Custer's Last Stand." This was the battle of June 25, 1876 between the Sioux and Cheyenne Indians and General George Custer's troop of men. Custer had underestimated the strength of the Indians, and he and his troops were destroyed.

There is a museum at the site, as well as a self-guilding auto tour. Military gravesites, including Custer's headstone, are also on display. For more information, you can call (800) 548-3390. If you want to write away for literature, address all correspondence to Travel Montana, Department of Commerce, Helena, Montana, 59620.

Yellowstone National Park

One of the most magnificent national parks, Yellowstone is famous for its spouting geysers, clear blue pools, percolating mud baths, tremendous mountains, and steep canyons. It is an all-around wonderland of nature.

Three of the five entrances to Yellowstone are in Montana—I-90, US 89, 191, and the Beartooth Highway (US 212). Open year-round, Yellowstone has 2,221,000 acres of breathtaking landscape.

The Yellowstone Institute offers about 50 seminars each year to aid visitors in becoming more knowledgeable about the Park and its wildlife and land. Courses are as diverse as geology, photography, and painting.

For more information about the Park, contact the Supervisor, Yellowstone National Park, Wyoming. For more information on the Yellowstone Seminars, write The Yellowstone Institute, Box 515, Yellowstone National Park, Mammoth, Wyoming, 82190, (307) 344-7381.

Nebraska

Boys Town

Father Flanagan's boys' home in Omaha is known worldwide. Founded in 1917 by a young Irish priest, Boys Town has been home to more than 15,000 young men. It is a self-contained village for residents, and it also has interesting attractions for visitors.

Father Flanagan's first home at Boys Town has been turned into a museum. Be sure also to visit the Father Flanagan Shrine. Another attraction, the Boys Town PhilaMatic Center, is one of the world's largest hobby museums. The "Oscar" that Spencer Tracy won for his role in the 1938 film "Boy's Town" resides there.

You should also try to see the Music Hall because you may be lucky enough to hear the famous Boys Town Choir rehearsing for its concert tour of the U.S.

The famous Two Brothers Statue is on the Boys' Town grounds. It has one boy carrying another on his back and is inscribed with those famous words "He ain't heavy, Father . . . He's m'brother."

One can visit Boys Town any time during the year. Call ahead for guided group tours. For more information, you can write Father Flanagan's Boys' Home, Boys Town, Nebraska, 68010, (402) 498-1350.

NEBRASKAland Days

Held the third week in June, NEBRASKAland Days is one of the state's most exciting events. Carrying on the tradition of Western hospitality that began with Buffalo Bill Cody, NEBRASKAland Days is a mixture of festivities, feasts, shows, rodeos, and parades.

There are sports competitions like the NEBRASKAland Days Road Run, tennis, softball, golf tournaments, and senior citizens' Olympics. Most everyone is dressed in Western garb. In fact, "arrests" are made for improper attire.

Big name entertainment graces the stage for 2 big shows each year. The penultimate event, however, is the Buffalo Bill Rodeo that has nearly 500 professional cowboys competing. Cowboys even ride buffalo. If you don't ride like a cowboy but just look like one, you can always enter the beard judging contest.

There are many motels in the North Platte area. There are also several campsites nearby. For more information, write the NEBRASKAland Days office, Box 706, North Platte, Nebraska, 69101.

Nebraska State Capitol

One of the top ten architectural wonders of the world, Nebraska's State Capitol Building in Lincoln consists of a majestic tower rising from a square base. The heart of the government resides in the building—the governor's offices, the state legislative body, and the State Supreme Court.

The lives of the early pioneers are depicted in three paintings in the vestibule—the Homesteader's Campfire, the First Furrow, and the Houseraising. The Great Hall contains beautiful mosaics that tell the story of important events in Nebraska's history. The three murals in the Rotunda are more symbolic, showing man laboring with his heart, hands, and head.

Nebraska's legislative body is located in the Rotunda. Try to observe a session of the Unicameral, Nebraska's one-house, non-partisan legislature. It's the only one of its kind in the nation.

Tours of the Capitol are given daily. For more information, you can write the Department of Administrative Services, State Building Division, Lincoln, Nebraska, 68509. Or call (402) 471-3191.

Nevada

Las Vegas

You must go to Las Vegas at least once in your life to experience the glitter and dazzle of the Strip. Opulent resort hotels and casinos, each more flashy than the next, line the street. When you're done playing the slots, check out a Las Vegas show or revue. Anyone who's anyone plays Las Vegas!

You can also head to downtown Las Vegas for more glittery marquises and casinos. Famous Fremont Street provides the Las Vegas background for many television shows and movies.

Las Vegas has recently built a Wet 'n Wild water theme amusement park. The $14 million project is part of an ongoing effort to create more family entertainment in Las Vegas. There are many exciting water activities like slides and flumes and plenty of opportunities for a good tan.

Tour the Liberace Museum for a first-hand look at "Mr. Showmanship's" legendary memorabilia. You can also view the 200 antique autos at the Imperial Place along the Strip.

For more information contact the Las Vegas Convention and Visitor's Authority, 3150 Paradise Road, Las Vegas, Nevada, 89109-9096, (702) 733-2200.

Cowboy Poetry Gathering

Over the last weekend in January, cowboys gather in Elko to recite their poetry, exhibit their art, and perform their music. Cowboy poetry developed because of the long stretches of time cowboys spent on the range. To help pass the time, they wrote poems and songs which they shared with other cowboys. With its rough edges and caustic wit, cowboy poetry is an American folk art.

More than 100 cowboy poets are expected to attend the festival. The only criterion is that these poets must have earned most of their living working with cattle at some point in their lives.

More than 50 poets are considered featured poets. However, there are open sessions for other cowboys and ranch people who want to share poetry at the festival.

Further information is available from the Gathering Offices. A list of books, cassette recordings and videotapes of cowboy poetry is available on request. For more details, contact Cowboy Poetry Gathering, Box 888, Elko, Nevada, 89801, (702) 738-7508.

Reno National Air Races

The second week in September, top airplane pilots flock to Reno for the annual Reno National Championship Air Races. It's a living aviation museum, energized by the spirit of flying.

One can see thundering World War II planes, P-38s arcing around straight-away pylons, wing walkers performing daredevil feats in the air. B-17s make low level passes right in front of your seats. You'll witness the fastest propeller machines in the world, and maybe even see a world record being broken.

There's always a flying machine in the air—whether it's homemade ultra-lights or Air Force jets. For more details, contact the Nevada Commission of Tourism, Capitol Complex, Carson City, Nevada, 89710, (702) 885-4322.

New Hampshire

Strawberry Banke

Strawberry Banke got its name from the abundance of wild berries found by the first English settlers. Today, Strawberry Banke is a living museum with 37 original historic buildings on ten acres. One of the nation's oldest neighborhoods, Strawberry Banke has period furnished homes that date from 1695 to 1945.

Walking through Strawberry Banke, one can see how the neighborhood evolved over 400 years of cultural change. There are many exhibits on social history, traditional trades, and architecture. There are beautiful gardens and fascinating archeological excavations. Artisans skilled in traditional crafts still manufacture and sell their goods.

In addition to regular exhibits and activities, Strawberry Banke offers monthly festivals and workshops ranging from the annual New England Gardening Day in June to the Christmastime Candlelight Stroll in December.

The museum is open daily, May through October. For more information, contact Strawberry Banke, P.O. Box 300, Portsmouth, New Hampshire, 03801, (603) 436-8010.

Mt. Washington Cog Railway

The Mt. Washington Cog Railway was built in 1866 as the world's first mountain climbing railway. After an hour and a half ride, you reach the summit of Mt. Washington and the Sherman Adams Observation Center. On a clear day you can see all 6 New England States. Before you board the train, stop off at the museum. You'll see the unique engineering design that allows a toothed-wheel to hook onto the center track and pull the steam engines up an incline as steep as 35 degrees.

Trains run hourly during the season which goes from mid-May to mid-October. The last train departs approximately 3 hours before sunset. Scheduling is always subject to weather conditions. For more information, contact Mt. Washington Cog Railway, Route 302, Bretton Woods, New Hampshire, (603) 846-5404.

The Flume

The Flume is one of New Hampshires most striking natural wonders. It is an 800-foot-long natural chasm with a spectacular waterfall. It is located in Franconia Notch State Park, a beautiful state park with trails for hiking and walking.

There are a variety of different trails that lead you to the Flume. And you can stop anywhere on route to view the Flume—you don't have to go to the top for terrific viewing.

The 70 foot moss-covered granite walls of the Flume and the glacial pools are also magnificent. There are also several lovely covered bridges near the Flume. They offer wonderful views and vistas. A visitor's center at the entrance to the Park has different exhibits on the history, geology and vegetation of the area.

Franconia Notch State Park is located in

Franconia, New Hampshire. The Flume is open May 25 to October 20 daily, 9-4 p.m. Tours are available and there is an admission fee, as well. If you have questions, call (603) 823-5563.

New Jersey

Cape May Beaches

For those who want beach resort amenities in a Victorian setting, the Cape May beaches are the ones to visit. Many presidents used to vacation here, and Cape May has retained that Victorian attention to detail. Hotels and inns have porch pillars and ornate railings, gables and woodcarvings.

At the tip of Cape May is the Cape May Lighthouse, the illuminated beacon for sea travellers many, many years ago. There are also other historical buildings such as the Cape May courthouse.

Over 1 million people visit the Cape May beaches to swim, to surf, to lay on the sand. You might consider visiting off-season when the crowds are less and the beaches still lovely. For more information, contact (609) 884-2159, ext. 28.

Atlantic City

Atlantic City has been a popular vacation spot since the civil war. These days, however, its lure is the glitter of the casinos as well as the sparkle of the beach.

The Casinos offer more than excitement at the tables or slots. They all have spectacular floor shows and big-name entertainment. Treat yourself to gourmet fare at the many fine restaurants. If you come in May, you may bump into a newly-crowned Miss America in the lobby, as the pageant is held in Atlantic City every year.

The six-mile Boardwalk is famous. You can take a tram ride down the ocean or bike it, if that's your preference. If you walk, you can shop as you stroll. The salt-water taffy is a must—whatever your mode of locomotion.

For more information on events in Atlantic City, contact the Atlantic City Convention and Visitor's Bureau, 16 Central Pier, Atlantic City, N.J., 08401, (609) 345-7546.

Washington Crossing State Park

This state park is a must for history buffs, as it marks the site of Washington's famous Delaware Crossing, Christmas night in 1776, which was a move that took the British by surprise.

You can visit the Ferry House, aboretum and open-air amphitheater. You can even fish in the Delaware River. Beautiful trails make wonderful day hikes or overnight camping trips. The park is also a great place to bird watch.

The Park is located off Route 29 in Washington Crossing. For more information, call (609) 292-6347.

New Mexico

International Balloon Fiesta
The first week in October marks the annual Albuquerque International Balloon Fiesta, humbly called the "really BIG one!" The largest hot air ballooning festival in the world, the Fiesta features more than 500 giant 7-story tall balloons.

Each day, the colorful balloons cover the sky. Pilots may perform a sort of balloon ballet, as several balloons ascend together. Spectators can also watch exciting competitions and races between balloonists. Aerial acrobatics by stunt pilots are thrilling to see.

All kinds of Southwestern souvenirs are also on sale—from Mexican pottery to Indian jewelery to stained glass with a strong balloon theme. You won't be disappointed if you're craving Southwestern eats either—there are ample supplies of breakfast burritos, Indian fry bread, and chili con carne.

The only thing you've got to remember to bring are a camera and film, although the balloon mass ascension is a sight you'll not soon forget. For more information, contact the Albuquerque Convention and Visitors Bureau, P.O. Box 26866, Albuquerque, New Mexico, 87125.

The Turquoise Trail
The Turquoise Trail is a route passing through

a series of ghost towns, once inhabited by people lured to New Mexico by hopes of gold and silver. The three towns—Golden, Madrid and Cerrillos—have been rediscovered by artisans who have renovated the old buildings.

New shops and restaurants occupy buildings that once stood empty of all but the collecting desert dust. Old Southwestern history intermingles with contemporary art to create an exciting environment, welcoming to all visitors. If you visit Madrid on a Sunday afternoon in the summer, chances are you can catch some pretty great jazz in the old ballpark.

The Turquoise Trail is located on North New Mexico 14, which is part of the "Scenic Route" to Santa Fe. For more information, contact the Albuquerque Convention and Visitors Bureau, P.O. Box 26866, Albuquerque, New Mexico, 87125.

Indian Pueblo Cultural Center

Celebrating the history of the Indian pueblo, the Cultural Center illustrates the evolution of Pueblo culture from prehistoric times to the present. The Cultural Center has exhibits on each of New Mexico's 19 Indian pueblos, suggesting both similarities and differences between them.

The permanent exhibit on the lower level concerns itself with a general history of the pueblo. The upper level has changing exhibits that feature contemporary Pueblo artists. Such art may include murals, silver work, or oils.

Plan on having lunch at the Center, as it's a great place to try traditional Native American foods such as Indian fry bread. Native dancing and craft demonstrations happen on weekends from May through October.

The Center is open daily, although it is closed on Sundays from mid-October through mid-May. For more information, contact the Indian Pueblo Cultural Center, 2401 Twelfth Street NW, Albuquerque, New Mexico. Call (505) 843-7270.

New York

Niagara Falls

The world's most accessible waterfall is one of the great natural wonders of the world. There are several different ways to get to the Falls—the Maid of the Mist boat takes you to its base; the Cave of the Winds takes you behind the waterfalls; and the Observation Tower's elevators lift you 100 feet above the thundering waters.

And there are several different ways to view the Falls, as well—stand behind the Falls at Terrapin and Prospect Points, be in the middle of it on Goat Island; or fly over the whole shebang in a helicopter.

All seasons are perfect to see the Falls. If you visit from late November to January, you'll receive a bit of a bonus as the downtown of Niagara becomes a "Festival of Lights."

For more information, contact the Chamber of Commerce in Niagara, New York. Or you can write the New York State Department of Commerce, One Commerce Plaza, Albany, New York, 12245.

Cooperstown

This 200 year old village in the Central region of New York pays homage both to America's first novelist (James Fenimore Cooper) and America's favorite pastime (baseball).

Reminders of Cooper and his family are all over

the town. Fenimore House is the ancestral home. It is now home to the New York State Historical Association and is filled with a fine collection of folk art and authentic period furnishings.

The Fenimore House is located on Otsego Lake, which was Cooper's famous "Glimmerglass." It is now a state park and houses a summer opera company.

When most people say "Cooperstown," they think baseball since Cooperstown is the home of the National Baseball Museum and Hall of Fame. It stands in tribute to the finest players and the thrills of more than a century of a sport that's said to have first been played in Cooperstown.

For more information, contact the Chamber of Commerce in Cooperstown, New York. Or you can write the New York State Department of Commerce, One Commerce Plaza, Albany, New York, 12245.

New York City

If you're anywhere in New York, you must visit the city that has been called the most exciting in the world. See the Statue of Liberty, located in Manhattan Harbor. Take the Staten Island Ferry and view it from the water—or climb to the top of the Statue herself.

Check out the South Street Seaport, where new shops and restaurants have revitalized an old fish market. Some of the world's best art is housed in museums like the Metropolitan Museum of Art or the Museum of Modern Art. Certainly, you can't come to New York and not see a Broadway show. Try Off Broadway if you're looking for something a little more avant-garde.

For more information, contact the Chamber of

Commerce in New York, New York. Or you can write the New York State Department of Commerce, One Commerce Plaza, Albany, New York, 12245.

North Carolina

Cape Hatteras National Seashore

The National Seashore stretches 75 miles along the open beach of the Outerbanks, the fragile barrier islands off the Carolina coast. Cape Hatteras also covers 30,000 acres of land on the islands of Bodie, Hatteras, and Dracoke. Because the land is all undeveloped, the beaches offer tremendous solitude and beauty.

Oracoke is infamously known as the site where Blackbeard the Pirate was killed. All three islands have lighthouses that are considered historical landmarks, although you are not allowed to climb the Bodie Island Lighthouse. At 208 feet, the Cape Hatteras Lighthouse is the tallest lighthouse in America. It offers a spectacular view of the Outerbanks.

The Cape Hatteras National Seashore is open for camping in the summer. An off-season visit is highly recommended to take advantage of the silent beauty of the beaches in the winter.

For more information on Cape Hatteras, contact the North Carolina Travel and Tourism Division, Department of Commerce, Raleigh, North Carolina, 27611.

The Blue Ridge Parkway

The National Park Service maintains over 250 miles of this road that travels the top of the mountains between the North Carolina-Virginia line and the entrance to the Great Smoky Mountains National Park near Cherokee.

The Parkway has many overlooks that provide spectacular views. There are also recreation areas that offer special exhibits on the history and geography of North Carolina. Trails, campgrounds, and picnic areas are available all along the Blue Ridge Road. The Moses Cone Memorial Park is one of the main recreational areas. In addition to trails and lakes and forests and deer, there is also a Manor house with a crafts center.

While the entire road is open from April 15 to November, some parts are closed during the winter months. For more information on the Blue Ridge Parkway, contact the North Carolina Travel and Tourism Division, Department of Commerce, Raleigh, North Carolina 27611.

North Carolina State Government Complex

Raleigh is the center of North Carolina's government and its history. As the state's capital, it contains five buildings that are key both to the state's history and to its government.

People consider the Governor's mansion, which was built during the mid-1800's, to be one of the finest examples of Victorian architecture in the country. The North Carolina Museum of History contains the original Carolina Charter. Other exhibits feature North Carolina's historical beginnings in the 16th century.

The State Legislative building sits on an entire city block and is the only building in the U.S. whose sole function on the state level is legislative. The North Carolina State Capitol was built in 1833 and is a perfect example of Greek Revival architecture. The office of the governor, it resides downtown on Capital Square.

For more information on the North Carolina State Government Complex, contact the North Carolina Travel and Tourism Division, Department of Commerce, Raleigh, North Carolina, 27611.

North Dakota

Theodore Roosevelt National Park

This park pays homage to Theodore Roosevelt whose presidential administration set up a national conservation policy. The area in and around the park is the North Dakota Badlands, a varying terrain of buttes, valleys and gorges.

All sorts of wildlife call the park home—buffalo, deer, antelope, wild horses, coyote, prairie dogs, and bobcats. The bald eagle and other wildlife also reside here. If you want to see wildlife, it's best to be in the park in the early morning or late evening.

The scenery in the park is spectacular, as is the plethora of wild flowers that cover the land. The park is located next to Medora, the restored pioneer cattle town. You can also enter the park 15 miles south of Watford City on Highway 18.

For more information, contact the Theodore Roosevelt National Park, P.O. Box 198, Medora, North Dakota, 58645, (800) 437-2070.

Norsk Hostfest

In late December, Minot hosts the Norsk Hostfest, a celebration of the Scandinavian culture. The Norsk Hostfest provides Scandinavians entry to their old culture through authentic foods, crafts, music, and dance.

American and Scandinavian musicians entertain throughout the festival. Scandinavian dignitaries also attend the Hostfest. Each day begins with a very moving flag ceremony that features the flags of all the Scandinavian countries.

You get a strong sense of Scandinavian culture in observing its arts and crafts. Artists demonstrate such crafts as rosemaling, quilting, spinning and blacksmithing. Sampling such treats as smorgasbord sandwiches, Danish Abelskivvers, sandbakkel, and sweet soup also provides a taste of the Scandinavian culture.

For more information, contact the Norsk Hostfest Association, P.O. Box 2111, Minot, North Dakota, 58702.

The North Dakota State Fair

For nine days in July, North Dakota throws itself a party, cloaked in the guise of a state fair. The fair features farm and craft exhibits, top entertainment, and the State Championship Finals Rodeo.

There are over 150 free entertainment shows, featuring mostly rock and country music and more than 600 commercial exhibits, generally suggesting the best way to operate a farm. The 4-H building houses more than 5000 exhibits. And, of course, there are tractor pulls, rodeos, auto races, and carnival attractions.

For more information, contact the North Dakota Tourism Promotion, Liberty Memorial Building, Capitol Grounds, Bismarck, ND, 58505, (701) 224-2525.

Ohio

The Pro-Football Hall of Fame

The Pro-Football Hall of Fame is a four-building complex paying homage to pro-football history. Exhibit areas, a football movie theater, a research library, a museum store, and the twin enshrinement halls complete the celebration of America's favorite fall sport.

The first thing one sees in entering the Hall is a seven-foot statue of the legendary Jim Thorpe. The Hall allows each NFL team its own exhibit in the Professional Football Today rooms. The Pro Football Art Gallery is another popular display. Every hour, a different football action film is screened in the Hall's movie theater.

Another exhibit chronicles the Super Bowl series in great detail. Two significant features of that exhibit are the Super Bowl Ring display and the highlights from championships past.

The Pro Football Hall of Fame is located in Canton and is open daily. For more information, contact The Pro-Football Hall of Fame, 2121 George Halas Drive, Canton, OH, 44708. You can call them at (216) 456-8207.

Air Force Museum

The world's largest military aviation museum, the Air Force Museum, contains antique airplanes, missiles, artifacts, and photographs—

spanning the period from Kitty Hawk to the present.

Over 100 aircraft are exhibited indoors along with hardware, documents, and personal memorabilia. About 60 other aircraft are housed in two hangars near the museum. These planes are in the process of being restored.

A research library that contains selected documents, photographs, and aircraft drawings exists in the museum. One can use these historical materials during weekdays only. The museum itself is open on weekends as well.

The museum is located near Dayton. For more information, contact Air Force Museum, Wright-Patterson AFB, Ohio, 45433, (513) 255-3284.

Sea World

The Mid-West's only marine life/zoological park, Sea World offers live shows that feature trained whales, dolphins and other sea animals. It is also the home of "Shamu," the killer whale.

Sea World is home to more than 100 penguins, too. Ice and man-made rock simulate an Arctic environment. 5000 pounds of fresh man-made snow are also critical to the penguin's habitat.

A Native Fishes of Ohio aquarium features endangered aquatic life. There is also a more general World of the Sea aquarium. Dolphins, seals, and sea lions have their own petting pools.

Sea World is located near Cleveland and is open from May 18 through September 8. For more information, write Sea World, 1100 Sea World Dr., Aurora, Ohio, (216) 562-8101.

Oklahoma

Discoveryland's "Oklahoma"

Discoveryland's outdoor amphitheater in Tulsa is the national home of Rodger's and Hammerstein's celebrated musical "Oklahoma." You've probably already seen the musical or the movie, but it's an entirely different experience when seen outdoors in its home state in a 2000 person amphitheater.

A western style barbeque with ribs and fixings is available before the show. Old fashioned snacks and desserts like Oklahoma "mud pies," berries and cream, and ice cold lemonade finish the meal.

Discoveryland's production of "Oklahoma" has won plaudits from national newspapers including the *New York Daily News* and the *San Diego Tribune*. Performances are nightly from June 2 to August 25. For more information, contact Discoveryland, 6711 S. Vale, Tulsa, OK, 74136, (918) 245-0242.

Will Rogers Memorial

The Will Rogers Memorial in Claremore houses the singing cowboy's memorabilia and documents his life as he grew to be one of America's best-loved humorists.

Exhibits include his saddle collection, dioramas of his life, showbills and posters, and a short film narrated by Rogers. On the grounds are several statues of Rogers, as well as his tomb site.

A new media center includes a small theater for viewing Rogers' films, a vault, a research library and preservation work rooms. The research library is open only by appointment.

For more information, contact the Will Rogers Memorial, P.O. Box 157, Claremore, OK, 74018, (918) 341-0719.

The State Fair of Oklahoma

Every September, Oklahoma sponsors a state fair that is one of the most lavish fairs in the nation. It features thrilling shows such as the Ice Capades, the Stock Car Races and the State Fair Rodeo.

The Fair is also known for its attention to aesthetic details and for its many sparkling fountains that offer soothing respite for weary fair-goers. A mono-rail provides an aerial view of the fair for its riders. The 330-foot Space Tower offers another bird's eye view of the fair, too.

Livestock exhibits, horse shows and made in Oklahoma products are just some of the exhibits of the fair. Outdoor exhibits include camping, forestry, fishing and mobile living.

Top-name entertainment give shows in the Grandstand. There are more than 150 free shows on the outdoor stages. This entertainment ranges from belly dancing to drill teams to karate demonstrations to gospel music to comedy.

For more information, contact The State Fair of Oklahoma, P.O. Box 74943, 500 Lake Rush Street, Oklahoma City, OK, 73147, (405) 942-5511.

Oregon

Oregon Shakespearean Festival

Tucked beneath the majestic Siskiyou Mountains, Ashland offers performances of Shakespearean and modern plays so fine that the theater won a 1983 Tony Award for "outstanding achievement in regional theater."

The season runs from February through October and offers works by playwrights as diverse as Eugene O'Neill, Luigi Pirandello, Christopher Durang and, of course, William Shakespeare. Ashland has three very different theaters in which to perform these plays, making the Ashland theatrical experience an even more special one.

The Elizabethan Stage has been designed to resemble London's Fortune Theatre, circa 1600, and is used primarily for the Shakespeare plays. The Angus Bowmer Theatre is a very modern theater in which the audience feels very much a part of the space they share with the actors. The Black Swan Theatre is the smallest and most personal of Ashland's three stages and is often used for Ashland's most avant-garde performances.

For more information, contact the Oregon Shakespearean Festival, 15 South Pioneer St., Box 158, Ashland, Oregon, 97520. You can call them at (503) 482-4331.

Washington Park

Washington Park is the perfect place for a family to spend a day together in Portland. You can smell the more than 10,000 rose bushes (a day's activity in itself) in the International Rose Test Gardens, stroll through the Japanese Gardens, and spend what's left of the day at the Washington Park Zoo.

The rose gardens bloom from mid-May until late November and are a favorite setting for photographers. Cross the road, and you enter the Japanese Gardens that recreate the serene beauty of ancient Japan.

A train is available to take visitors from the gardens to the zoo. The zoo is particularly known for its elephants: more Asian elephants have been raised in this zoo than anywhere outside of the Asian wilds. The zoo also offers hands-on exhibits and nature trails featuring the wildlife of the Cascade mountain region.

The Japanese Gardens and Zoo are open all year round. For more information, contact the Oregon Economic Development Department, 595 Cottage Street NE, Salem, Oregon, 93710.

Mt. Hood National Forest

Mt. Hood, Oregon's tallest mountain, offers year-round activities for skiers, mountain climbers, and hikers. Easily accessible from Portland, the Mt. Hood Loop route is considered one of the Northwest's most scenic drives.

As you drive, you'll follow the Clackamas River, which offers plenty of fishing, swimming and white water experiences. Drive a bit more and you'll come across the Northwest's only alpine slide, located at one of the mountain's five ski areas.

Timberline Lodge is, perhaps, the most famous structure on Mount Hood. It received Historic Landmark status since it was built as a WPA project in the early 1930's. Even if you're not a skier, you can ride the Magic Mile chairlift and witness the spectacular vistas that Mt. Hood affords.

For more information contact the Oregon Economic Development Department, 595 Cottage Street NE, Salem, Oregon, 93710.

Pennsylvania

Independence National Historical Park

Independence Park in Philadelphia has been called "the most historical square mile in America." Independence Hall, built in the mid-1700's, was the site of some of the most important events in U.S. history—George Washington received the title of commander-in-chief of the Continental Army in 1775; the Declaration of Independence was adopted in 1776; the Articles of the Confederation were accepted in 1783; and the Constitution was penned in 1787.

Independence Hall used to house the Liberty Bell, but it moved across the street in 1983 to the Liberty Bell Pavilion. Another historical jewel in the Park's crown is Franklin Court, which celebrates Ben Franklin's life. The court consists of a steel-frame outline of Franklin's house, a restoration of an 18th century print shop, and an architectural archeological exhibit. There is also an underground museum that details the major events of Franklin's life.

More than 20 historical sites occupy space on this square mile in downtown Philadelphia. All are free. For more information, contact the Philadelphia Convention and Visitor's Bureau, 3 Penn Center Plaza, Philadelphia, PA, 19102, (215) 636-3300.

White River Rafting

There are three areas for great white river rafting in Pennsylvania—the Youghiogheny, the Lehigh, and Pine Creek Gorge. All 3 provide available guides, equipment, rental, and a terrific run through the rapids.

"The Yough" takes you 7 miles through Ohiopyle State Park. Powerful rapids and spectacular scenery make for an unforgettable river ride. The Lehigh offers a tamer 12 1/2 mile Upper Gorge run or a more hairy 18 mile Lower Gorge trip. Either choice gives you a good paddle. Pine Creek has gentler water than the others, but the rapids still give plenty of white water excitement.

For more information, you should contact the Pennsylvania Department of Commerce, Bureau of Travel Development, 416 Forum Building, Harrisburg, PA, 17120, (717) 787-5453.

Springs Folk Festival

Early October, the tiny Amish and Mennonnite village of Springs in Somerset County puts on a folk festival that celebrates pioneer and mountain arts and crafts. The Pennsylvania Dutch may call themselves "the Plain People," but their cultural heritage is beautifully rich.

People demonstrate crafts like glassblowing and quilting. Pennsylvania Dutch objects, fraktur, and furniture are also on display. It's no surprise that the festival reflects the Pennsylvania Dutch love of hearty food, too. How can you resist the smell of apple butter cooking in a big copper crock?

For more information, contact Penn Alps, Inc., Grantsville, Maryland, 21536, (301) 895-5985.

Rhode Island

Hammersmith Farm

On fifty rolling acres overlooking Narragansett Bay, Hammersmith Farm is one of Newport's most majestic mansions and its only remaining working farm. Established in 1640, it was purchased by John Auchincloss as a family retreat in 1887. And it was he who built the 28 room shingle style cottage.

Hammersmith Farm achieved national prominence in the late 1950's when Jacqueline Bouvier wed John F. Kennedy there. Visitors can tour the rooms and the grounds. The gardens were designed by Frederick Law Olmstead, who is responsible for Central Park in New York City. The lawns and meadows stretch down to the bay where the presidential yacht, "Honey Fitz," was docked when President Kennedy visited.

Guided tours are available daily April through October. The estate is open weekends in March and November. For more information contact Hammersmith Farm, Ocean Drive, Newport, Rhode Island, 02840, (401) 846-0402.

Blithewold Gardens and Arboretum

One of New England's most exquisite landscape gardens, Blithewold Gardens and Arboretum was once the summer residence of coal tycoon Augustus Van Winkle. Exotic trees and shrubs from Europe and Asia dot the grounds.

All trees are labelled, and some of the more exciting ones include Chinese toon trees, ginkgos, Japanese tree lilacs, and a grove of bamboo. An outstanding feature of the garden is an eighty foot tall giant Sequoia, the tallest tree of this kind east of the Rockies.

The flower gardens are located throughout the grounds and are quite spectacular. Many of the flowers are rare, and all have been chosen to complement the beautiful view of the Narragansett Bay that you have from the garden.

The Gardens are open all year round, but the mansion is open from May to October only. For more information, contact Blithewold Gardens and Arboretum, Ferry Rd., Bristol, Rhode Island, 02809, (401) 253-8714.

Block Island

A mere 12 miles out to sea, Block Island is a Victorian hamlet, surrounded by gently rolling countryside and stone fences. The island is accessible by ferry. Once there, most people tend to get around by bicycle. The harbor area represents the island's only village—with shops, restaurants, and inns. The beaches are magnificent, both those on the Atlantic Ocean and those on Block Island Sound.

There are plenty of opportunities for hiking, as there are many carefully maintained nature trails. The island also has five wildlife refuges. One of the trails on the island brings you to the Bluffs. At 200 feet above the ocean, you've got a tremendous view of the Atlantic and the Rocky Shoreline below.

For more information, contact The Block Island Chamber of Commerce, Drawer D, Block Island, Rhode Island, 02807, (401) 466-2436.

South Carolina

Myrtle Beach

South Carolina offers 55 miles of public beach along the Atlantic Ocean. The strip of shore is called the Grand Stand, and Myrtle Beach is probably the biggest drawing card. The capital of fun in the sun, Myrtle Beach has gorgeous beaches, terrific fishing, superb golfing, and amusements for the entire family.

The beaches are quite wide, which makes them idea for picking up shells, strolling the sands, or catching a tan. Surf casting is very popular off the beaches. Many people also fish off the piers or go deep-sea fishing.

If you're looking for non-beach related entertainment, you should check out the Ripley's Believe It or Not Museum or the Guinness Hall of Records in the middle of the town on North Ocean Boulevard. The Myrtle Beach Pavilion is the heart of the Grand Strand's amusement area. Its centerpiece is the largest flume ride in the Carolinas.

The Myrtle Beach State Park is also very popular. Cabins, camping, swimming, hiking, fishing—all are easily available. The Park is located on U.S. 17. You should write ahead for cabin reservations. Contact them at Myrtle Beach State Park, Myrtle Beach, South Carolina, 29577, (803) 238-5325.

For more information on Myrtle Beach

attractions, contact the Myrtle Beach Area Chamber of Commerce, 1301 N. King's Highway, P.O. Box 2115, Myrtle Beach, South Carolina, 29578-2115, (803) 626-7444.

Fort Moultrie/Fort Sumter

Two historically great forts anchor the Charleston harbor. Fort Moultrie which was critical to the Patriots' cause during the Revolutionary War, and Fort Sumter, which received the first shot fired during the civil war.

Fort Moultrie has defended Charleston Harbor for over 200 years, and visitors can tour it on Sullivan's Island. Relive Sergeant William Jasper's heroic attempt to replace the torn Palmetto flag as British cannon fire rained around him. This national monument is also the burial site of General William Moultrie who built the fort, and Osceola, the Seminole Indian Chief. Admission to Fort Moultrie is free.

Fort Sumter is considered one of the most historically significant military sites in the U.S. It was here that the first shots of the civil war were fired as Fort Sumter received fire from Fort Johnson. Fort Sumter saw tremendously harsh and bloody fighting. Its ravaged structure was restored after the war, and it is now under the supervision of the National Parks Service. You can take a boat tour of the monument. Boats leave from the City Marina.

For more information, contact the Charleston County Park, Recreation and Tourist Commission, 172 Meeting St., P.O. Box 834, Charleston, SC, 29402, (800) 845-7108.

McKissick Museums of the University of South Carolina

The McKissick Library Building houses the University's galleries and museums. Located opposite Sumter Street, the building is on the University Horseshoe which dates back to the early 18th century when the University received its charter.

The museums contain art exhibits, a collection of cut gemstones, a geology exhibit, and Bernard Baruch's antique silver collection. The first floor of the Museum contains the Movietonews Film Library. This library houses more than 60 million feet of news film that captures the world between 1919 and 1963.

For more information, contact the Greater Columbia Chamber of Commerce, P.O. Box 1360, Columbia, SC, 29202, (603) 779-5350.

South Dakota

Mount Rushmore

Perhaps the greatest national monument, the greatest testament to the meaning and scope of America, is Mt. Rushmore, the heroic mountain sculptures of Washington, Jefferson, Lincoln, and Roosevelt.

Gazton Borglum began sculpting Mt. Rushmore in 1927 and died before completing his work. While he had finished the heads of the four presidents, he had initially intended to carve them to their waists. The presidents' heads are more than 60 feet high, scaled to men whose height would measure 465 feet tall. The noses are 20 feet long, and the eyes 11 feet wide.

The carry out his pioneer project, Borglum used innovative sculpture techniques—dynamite and jackhammers. He supervised work from a cable-supported basket which brought him quickly from top to bottom.

Mt. Rushmore is located in the Black Hills and is open daily, all year round. From May to September, there are special programs including tours of Borglum's studio. For more information, contact the Superintendent, Mt. Rushmore Memorial, Keystone, South Dakota, 57751, (800) 843-1930.

Badlands National Park

There is nowhere in the world like The Badlands, with its world of sharp ridges, steepwalled canyons, gullies, pyramids and knobs covered by the whitish layer of ancient volcanic sea.

Although it is hard for animals to live in this steeply eroded terrain, the Badlands National Park is the site of fossil beds of animals from the Oligocene Epoch to the Age of Mammals. Badlands National Park has a herd of 300 bison in the Sage Creek Wilderness Area.

The park is open all year round, although most people visit during the spring, summer and fall. Winter camping, however, can offer majestic sights of snow-peaked canyons. Be aware that blizzards may often temporarily shut down roads. Backpackers are urged to consult with a ranger before heading off into the back country. For more information, contact the Superintendent, Badlands National Park, Interior, South Dakota, 57750.

Custer State Park

For an outstanding sampling of the Black Hills terrain, you must visit Custer State Park. There are hills and valleys, streams and lakes, and trees and grasses. Mt. Coolidge, at 6023 feet, is the tallest point in the park.

Bison flourish, playing a critical part in the park's ecocystem. You can also find bighorn sheep and mountain goats. Elk and deer run free, sometimes accompanied by extremely friendly burros. More than 180 species of birds live in the park, as well.

Campgrounds are scattered throughout the park—available on a first-come, first-served basis. There are well-marked trails for hiking and riding, and all lakes are open for fishing. The Park is open from May 1 to September 30. For more information, contact South Dakota Department of Game, Fish, and Parks, Division of Custer State Park, Star Route 3, Box 70, Custer, South Dakota, 57730, (605) 255-4515.

Tennessee

Graceland
What would a visit to Tennessee be like without a stop at Graceland, Elvis Presley's mansion in Memphis? Even if you're not an Elvis fan, it's a piece of Americana that's not to be missed—particularly in mid-August, during the International Elvis Tribute Week.

Built in 1939, Graceland was purchased by Elvis in 1957 and has been restored to reflect the period of his marriage to Priscilla Presley. Tours of the 14 acre, 18 room mansion last a full two hours. Only seven rooms are open to the public. The highlight may be Elvis' favorite room, appropriately named the Jungle Room, which features an African motif.

His carport houses flashy motorcycles and cars and features two Stutz Blackhawks, a Ferrari, and his mother's '55 pink Cadillac. Thousands of personal effects are also on display —including a replica of his 5-tiered wedding cake. There is also a 12-minute multi-media show featuring rare footage of Elvis in concert and at home.

For more information about Graceland, contact the Department of Tourist Development, Room T, Box 23170, Nashville, Tennessee, 37202, (615) 741-7994.

Opryland USA

More than 2 million people visit Opryland USA, a unique theme park dedicated to all types of American music. There are more than a dozen shows in the park, featuring a live orchestra, a variety of singers, dancers, and entertainers. For further entertainment, Opryland USA also offers the latest and most exciting thrill rides.

Several years ago, Opryland USA premiered a $3.7 million attraction called the Screamin' Delta Demon, one of the most thrilling (and that's an understatement) roller coasters in the world—a bobsled on wheels. Another popular park attraction is the Grizzly River Rampage, a white water raft ride.

Another not to be missed sight is the Conservatory, a 2-acre garden under glass. Jungle ravines, flowing streams and waterfalls, and 8000 plants and trees comprise this modern day Garden of Eden at the Opryland Hotel.

For more information about Opryland USA, contact the Department of Tourist Development, Room T, Box 23170, Nashville, Tennessee, 37202, (615) 741-7994.

Great Smoky Mountains National Park

On the Tennessee-North Carolina border, the Appalachian Mountain Range is cloaked in an ever-present bluish haze, giving rise to the name "Smoky Mountains." Sixteen peaks within the park soar above 6000 feet, and there are more than 700 miles of horse and hiking trails.

If you reach the top of 6593-foot Mount LeConte, you'll be rewarded with a stay at LeConte Lodge and a spectacular sunrise over the mountain wilderness. The park offers a wonderful variety of plant life with more than 1400 species of flowering plants.

The park also offers something for those who would prefer to tour by auto. The Foothills Parkway is a beautiful road. Some of the best views are reached by paved pathways less than a half mile off the road. The Park is open all year round. Each season colors the park with its own particular charm.

For more information about the Smoky Mountain National Park, contact the Department of Tourist Development, Room T, Box 23170, Nashville, Tennessee, 37202, (615) 741-7994.

Texas

The Alamo

Once a Spanish mission in downtown San Antonio, the Alamo is Texas's pre-eminent historical attraction. In 1836, it became the "Cradle of Texas Liberty," when a band of less than 200 Texas volunteers held off a skilled Mexican army of thousands for 13 days.

All the Alamo defenders died resisting the advances of Mexico's dictator Santa Ana—among them such heros as Davy Crockett and Jim Bowie. Although the Mexicans defeated the Texans at the Alamo, the cost to their army was dear, and Sam Houston routed their army at the Battle of San Jacinto.

The Alamo is open year-round, 9:30-5:00. For more information, contact the Texas Tourist Development Agency, P.O. Box 12008 Capitol Station, Austin, TX, 78711.

Big Bend National Park

Big Bend National Park is one of the most striking national parks in the country because of its extraordinarily varied terrain. The verdant vegetation of the Rio Grande flood plain contracts greatly with the expansive Chihuahuan Desert. Big Bend also includes the high country of the Chisos Mountains.

The Park is easily accessible either by car or

foot. One can take in the atmosphere of old Mexico by visiting the villages of Boquillas and Santa Elena, which are magnificently set off against the Sierra del Carmen and Fronteriza mountain ranges. The hiking trails vary from the 2-mile self-guided Lost Mine Trail to the much longer desert trails which circumnavigate the Chisos Mountains.

The park is open year-round. If you desire accommodations more plush than a tent, you should check out the Chisos Mountain Lodge, 5400 feet above sea level. For more information, contact the National Park Concessions, Inc., Big Bend National Park, Texas, 79834, (915) 477-2291.

Padre Island
Padre Island stretches 113 miles along the Texas Gulf Coast, a classic example of a barrier island formed by wave action and crowned by wind-formed dunes.

The coastal waters of Texas are warm-enough for swimming year-round, making the beaches a mighty attractive spot. The island also draws non-human visitors as it is home to more than 350 species of birds, including the great blue herons, sandering, gulls, and terns.

Mammals such as coyotes and gophers coexist with marine loggerhead turtles and a variety of different snakes. The fishing off Padre Island is excellent with certain species being more plentiful at certain seasons. October through March, for example, is the time to catch red snapper.

For more information on Padre Island, contact the Superintendent of Padre Island, 9405 S. Padre Island Dr., Corpus Christi, TX, 78418, (512) 937-2621.

Utah

Bryce Canyon National Park

To be precise, Bryce Canyon is not a canyon at all—but a series of rifts that drop 1000 feet through the limestone layers of 12 large amphitheaters. Nature has shaped delicate columns, spires, and windows and produced a breathtaking creation. Different species of trees at different elevations highlight the different colored limestone striations.

One can see the main geological attractions from overlooks along the paved roads, but the best way to see the park is on foot or horseback. Trails vary from 1/2 mile to 23 miles. The park and its visitor's center are open year round.

For more information, contact Superintendent, Bryce Canyon National Park, Bryce Canyon, Utah, 84717, (801) 834-5322.

Rainbow Bridge National Monument

One of the largest known natural bridges, Rainbow Bridge National Monument is one of the seven natural wonders of the world. Striking in its color and symmetry, the bridge stretches to a height of 290 feet and a width of 270 feet across.

One can walk or ride to the Rainbow Bridge from the Navajo Trading Post. However, most people prefer the water route, approaching by boat on Lake Powell. If you boat 50 miles from Wahweap Marina to the Bridge Canyon landing, you can then walk the remaining 1/2 mile to the bridge.

There are no picnic areas or campgrounds set aside within the monument area. Page, Arizona, is the site of the nearest services. For more information, contact the Superintendent, Glen Canyon National Recreation Area, Box 1507, Page, Arizona, 86040, (602) 745-2471.

Park City Ski Area

Some people say the powder in Utah is the best in the world, and Park City is Utah's largest ski area. It also possesses the West's longest gondola ride.

A skier has 2200 acres of skiable terrain before him as well as 650 acres of powder bowl skiing. Park City has trails for skiers of all abilities. If you haven't had your fill by the time the sun sets, Park City also offers night-skiing too.

In the summer, the Gondola takes visitors to the summit of Park City, allowing both skiers and non-skiers to experience the spectacular view. As you ride, notice the old weathered mining buildings scattered amongst the fir trees.

For more information on Park City's offerings, contact the Park City Chamber of Commerce/Convention and Visitor's Bureau, 528 Main Street, Park City, Utah, (800) 453-1360.

Vermont

Shelburne Museum and Heritage Park

35 historical buildings set on 45 rolling acres house what the New England Arts Council has called "the best collection of Americana in New England." The museums and park reflect the vision of Electra Havemeyer Webb. Her outstanding collection includes the historical buildings she had moved to Shelburne to showcase her Americana.

Three art galleries contain the exquisite paintings of Rembrandt, Monet, Degas, and Wyeth. Another building shelters a 525-foot scale model circus parade. Still others have beautiful antique furniture in their proper historical settings—including an authentic apothecary and doctor's office.

If you enjoy Americana, you'll be intrigued by the variety of quilts, dolls, scrimshaw, weathervanes, decoys, and carved eagles. A separate barn holds carriages, wagons, and sleighs. A one-room schoolhouse comes complete with century-old schoolwork hanging on the walls. A 220-foot steam paddlewheeler rests on the grounds, as does a lighthouse and typical Vermont covered bridge.

The museums are located in Shelburne, just south of Burlington. They are open mid-May to late October, 9-5. For more information, contact the Shelburne Museum, Shelburne, Vermont, 05482, (802) 985-3344.

Fall Foliage

Nowhere is Nature's color palette so striking as in Vermont's autumn leaves. Gorgeous reds, yellows, and oranges paint the countryside from the middle of September to the middle of October. It's hard to predict the exact color schemes of any one time. The leaves change at different times in different parts of the state. Generally, the leaves tend to change in early September in the more northern parts of Vermont. The seasonal transformation then moves southward. Peak color viewing is thought to be mid-season when you can see the greatest varieties of colors.

Since Vermont is only about 180 miles long, you can travel to a new spot if the colors are ahead or behind you at any point in time. Any local chamber of commerce will help travelers find housing during foliage tours. For more specific information, you can contact the Vermont State Chamber of Commerce, Box 37, Granger Road, Montpelier, Vermont, 05602, (802) 223-3443.

Skiing

If you drive 3 hours to touch Vermont's top and bottom, she'll offer you nearly 30 downhill ski areas and 50 ski touring centers. The Green Mountains of Vermont are anything but that color during the winter months—and the alpine resorts have ski trails for all abilities. Skiers who can ski the trails of Vermont can ski anywhere in the world.

Many of the alpine resorts offer ski packages—including lift tickets, lessons, and even child-care, if need be. They generally have extensive snow-farming techniques so there's no need to worry about snow conditions—even if Nature's not been particularly cooperative.

Natural snow fall is more important for Nordic ski-touring centers. They, too, provide challenges for all abilities of skiers as they generally have machine-groomed and track-set trails. Both Nordic and Alpine ski experiences allow you to participate in Vermont's natural beauty. The Alpine experience provides exquisite panoramic views, while the Nordic route envelops you in this beauty.

For more information about skiing in Vermont, contact the Vermont Travel Division, 134 State Street, Montpelier, Vermont, 05602, (802) 828-3236. The Vermont Snow Hotline is (802) 229-0531.

Virginia

Virgina Beach

Virginia Beach has long been the prime choice for vacationers wanting the Eastern Seaboard. While the surf and sand are top-notch, Virginia Beach also offers a variety of recreational activities for those wanting a break from traditional beach activities.

The Boardwalk has many bicycle rental shops. A two-wheeler can quickly put you on the City's 10-mile Virginia Beach Bikeway. It will also allow you to travel to the Seashore State Park and take advantage of the bike trails there.

The 17th Street Pier is a fisherman's delight. But fishermen can also be found surf-casting and trolling around sunken ships or on off-shore reefs. More than 22 species of fish call Virginia Beach waters home.

Golfers and tennis players have it made in Virginia Beach as well. The city has five 18-hole courses that are open to the public, and more than 130 public tennis courts.

For more information, contact the Virginia Division of Tourism, 202 North Ninth Street, Suite 500, Richmond, Virginia, 23219, (804) 786-2051.

Colonial Williamsburg

Colonial Williamsburg blends 18th century Virginia atmosphere with 20th century accessibility and welcomes visitors to this historic town of homes, churches, museums, and fife and drum corps.

Colonial Williamsburg has just reconstructed an 18th century hospital that was the first free-standing hospital designed for the mentally ill. Another recent addition is the DeWitt Wallace Decorative Arts Gallery that houses many colonial treasures.

Other major exhibits include the Public Gaol, authentic taverns, and several colonial homes. Bruton Parish Church, one of America's oldest churches, has been a site for worship since 1775.

For more information about Williamsburg, contact the Virginia Division of Tourism, 202 North Ninth Street, Suite 500, Richmond, Virginia, 23219, (804) 786-4484.

Mount Vernon

Mount Vernon, George Washington's plantation, may very well be the most famous house in America. Located on the Potomac, its 30 acres of pasture and gardens reflect the detailed planning with which Washington designed his estate.

Recently redecorated, Mount Vernon is a beautiful example of mid-Georgian architecture. Many original furnishings are on display. The 14 exhibit rooms are painted in the lush verdigris green, Prussian blue, and patent yellow that Washington originally wanted.

Two other Mount Vernon museums are on the grounds and are authentically furnished as well. For more information about Mount Vernon, contact the Virginia Division of Tourism, 202 North Ninth Street, Suite 500, Richmond, Virginia, 23219, (804) 786-4484.

Washington

Puget Sound Ferry

For a terrific way to experience the Puget Sound, take one of the Washington State ferries. The ferry system connects many different points in the Sound, and all routes offer superb scenery and views.

The San Juan Islands bring one back to the time of the Spanish explorations. 172 jewel-like islands lie scattered through the sound. An especially interesting ferry ride takes one through these islands to Sidney, British Columbia. Orcas Island offers an extraordinary view from the summit of Mt. Constitution.

Cross-sound rides are also popular for those with less time to spend on a boat. It's smart to avoid eastbound morning travel and westbound evening travel, so as not to get caught up in rush-hour traffic.

For schedules, rates, and travel ideas, contact Washington State Ferries, Colman Dock, Seattle, WA, 98104, (206) 464-6400.

Mount St. Helens

Until May 1980, Mount St. Helens appeared like her sister volcanoes in the Cascade mountain range—quiet and symmetrical. Her extraordinary eruption, however, has changed the landscape and offered living testament to the forces that originally shaped this part of the country.

You can visit the volcano, stopping off at the Mount St. Helens Visitor's Center or National Volcanic Monument Headquarters before winding your way up the volcano. There is hiking and camping in the area. It is recommended that you not drink the water, however.

There are many viewpoints along the way that offer different perspectives of the volcano. Certain points also allow you a view of nearby Mount Ranier.

For more information, you can call the Mount St. Helens National Volcanic Monument Headquarters, (206) 247-5473.

Museum of History and Industry

The Museum of History and Industry is like a time machine that takes you back to the 19th century Pacific Northwest—the time of the pioneers, sailors, loggers.

You are brought back to Seattle when it was first being settled. The museum has reconstructed a model of the streets of 1880 Seattle. The display features authentic commercial products and industry tools that people of that era would have used.

Other exhibits include the fashions of another era, the splendor of the Northwest's Gay Nineties. Another gallery specializes in maritime displays. It includes an exemplary selection of Puget Sound-related memorabilia.

The museum is open April to September, although it is open only on weekends in April, May, and September. For more information, contact Museum of History and Industry, 2700 24th Avenue East, Seattle, Washington, 98112, (206) 324-1125.

Washington, DC

National Air and Space Museum
The National Air and Space Museum is the most visited museum in the world—and it's easily understood why. Its 23 galleries represent the fascinating history of aviation and feature the exciting development of space technology. Specific exhibits include the original 1903 Wright Flyer, Lindbergh's Spirit of St. Louis, John Glenn's Friendship 7 space capsule, the Apollo 11 command module, and a space station.

The 50-feet high by 70-feet wide screen of the Langley Theatre makes a viewer feel as if he is right in the middle of the action of the exciting film being shown. No space museum would be complete without a planetarium—and this one offers special exhibits, as well.

The museum is open daily and admission is free. It is located on L'Enfant Plaza. For more information, call (202) 357-1400.

Washington Monument
Built in 1885 to honor the first president of the United States, the Washington Monument remains the tallest masonry structure in the world at 555 feet. Needless to say, this magnificent obelisk looms over every other building in the city of Washington.

If you climb (the elevator is free!) to the top of the monument, you get a perfect view of

Washington and its surrounding areas. Nothing impedes the view since there has been a 90 foot limit on building height in the city since 1889.

The monument is open daily from 9 to 5. However, the monument stays open 'til midnight during the summer. For more information, contact the Washington, DC Convention and Visitors Association, 1575 I Street, NW, Washington, DC, 20005, (202) 789-7007.

U.S. Capitol

The building where U.S. Senators and U.S. Representatives gather to enact national legislation is capped by a 180-foot sparkling white dome. Tours of the building not only include opportunities to view the magnificent architecture close-up but an opportunity to see the legislators in action, as well.

One first walks through majestic 10-ton bronze doors, designed by Randolph Rogers. Stop awhile and gaze at the Rotunda, painted by Constantino Brumidi. Statuary Hall includes two particular statues from each state.

In viewing the House of Representatives, one is struck by its size. In fact, it is the largest legislative chamber in the world. The tour also features the Senate and the Crypt which was the original site of the Supreme Court Chamber.

The Capitol building is open daily from 9 to 4:30, with extended summer hours. Admission and tours are free. For more information, contact the Washington, DC Convention and Visitors Association, 1575 I Street, NW, Washington, DC, 20005, (202) 789-7007.

West Virginia

Harper's Ferry National Historical Park

Harper's Ferry was the site of John Brown's illfated plan to liberate the slaves via insurrection in 1859. Today, it is a living example of 19th century life.

Tours and demonstrations offer the visitor opportunities to visualize the old Armory complex and understand the John Brown raid. "Union" soldiers in proper military dress give a sense of military life and explain the role Harper's Ferry played in the civil war. Other townspeople dressed in period costume further support the feeling of Harper's Ferry as living history.

There are several hiking trails within the park, all of which offer lovely forays into the West Virginia wilderness. For more information, write the Superintendent, Box 65, Harper's Ferry, West Virginia, 25425.

New River Gorge Bridge

Up until 1977, it was impossible to cross New River Gorge without detouring greatly and winding one's way down narrow mountain roads. 1977, however, marked the completion of the New River Gorge Bridge, the world's longest single arch steel span.

The length of the bridge is over 3000 feet and the arch is 1700 feet. It rises 360 feet in the air, the second highest bridge in the country. There is a Visitor's Center with an overlook that provides great views of the bridge and gorge.

On the second Saturday of October, the bridge is closed to auto traffic. That is the only day when pedestrians can walk across the bridge and view the gorge from above. For more information, contact Superintendent, New River Gorge National River, P.O. Drawer V, Oak Hill, West Virginia, 25901.

Canaan Valley Resort State Park
This Allegheny Mountain resort offers all sorts of activities all-year round. Winter guests can choose alpine (downhill) or nordic (cross-country) skiing. If you're not a skier, there's a beautiful rink for ice-skating.

Summer activities include lots of golf and tennis, as well as biking, hiking, fishing and hay rides. There's even a chairlift to take you to the top of the mountain for a gorgeous view of the valley.

Canaan Valley has a lodge with more than 250 rooms. Shades campsites are also available for those desiring a more rugged vacation. For more information, contact Canaan Valley Resort State Park, Route One, Box 39, Davis, West Virginia, 26260, (304) 866-4121.

Wisconsin

House on the Rock

Thousands of tourists visit this extremely intriguing sight—a fantastic house built on a rock pinnacle. The house holds a great collection of musical machines and artifacts, including the world's largest carousel.

The house features a "Streets of Yesterday" display in which visitors wind their way through a maze of authentic instruments and music boxes. Many of these musical machines were once part of royal collections. An underground area features different pipe organs and huge copper vats.

The House on the Rock is located off Highway 23 in Spring Green. For more information, you can call (608) 935-3639.

Experimental Aircraft Association (EAA) Fly-In

Every summer, Oshkosh hosts the annual Experimental Aircraft Association (EAA) Fly-In that draws thousands of spectators and pilots from all over the world. The week-long event includes many exciting air shows. The Fly-In is also noteworthy for the hundreds of experimental aircraft that line Oshkosh's Wittman Field.

Oshkosh itself is home to the Wisconsin Aviation Hall of Fame which is also located on Wittman Field. The EAA has a brand-new museum located in Franklin that features 200 military, historic, sport and home-made aircraft. It also archives photos, films, and other such aeronautic memorabilia.

For more information, contact the Experimental Aircraft Association, Box 229, Hales Corners, Wisconsin, 53130, (414) 425-4860.

Wisconsin Dells

One of the prettiest parts of Wisconsin, the Wisconsin Dells are best seen via boat trip down the Wisconsin River. Not only do the Dells offer terrific scenic beauty, but the area also provides other amusements, attractions, and fun.

Kids will love the amusement parks in the area. And the whole family will enjoy the evening water show on the river. You should also make sure you catch the Stand Rock Indian Ceremonial performed by the local Winnebago Indians. The Dells are also known for having some of the best food in the Midwest.

For more information, contact the Wisconsin Dells Regional Chamber of Commerce, Box 175, Wisconsin Dells, Wisconsin, 53965, (608) 254-8086.

Wyoming

Grand Teton National Park

The Grand Tetons in Western Wyoming have been called the "American Alps" because of the mountains' majesty. Unlike nearby Yellowstone, the Teton range was not formed by volcanic action—but is rather a great fault-block of rock. The entire area of the Park is nearly 500 square miles.

The Teton region is rich in wildlife. More than 60 species of animals can be found. Moose and elk are the most common. If you're a bird watcher, sighting a trumpeter swan is a great treat. The fishing is terrific, too—trout swim in both the Snake River and Jackson Lake, a great glacier lake.

The Grand Tetons offer trails for all sorts of hikers. Horses are also available for short rides and pack trips into the back country. The season for mountain climbing runs June through September. Snowmobiles and ski-touring treks let you experience the quiet beauty of the Park in winter.

For more information on the Grand Teton National Park, call (307) 733-2880.

Cheyenne Frontier Days

The Granddaddy of all rodeos, Cheyenne Frontier Days takes place the last week in July each year. The rodeo includes events such as bull riding, bareback and saddle bronc riding, bull-dogging, and the spectacular wild horse race.

Cheyenne Frontier Days is more than simply a rodeo, however. There are special parades that bring onlookers right back to the days of the Old West. Old-time carriages, automobiles, Indians, and country bands contribute to the flavor of another era. Nightly entertainment features big-time stars.

Another must for the Cheyenne Frontier Days attendee is the daily chuckwagon breakfasts. The fair also sponsors square dancing and Indian dancing to add to the flavor of the old West.

For more information on the Cheyenne Frontier Days, contact the Wyoming Travel Commission, I-25 at College Dr., Cheyenne, Wyoming, 82002-0660, (800) 553-2784.

Fort Lamarie

Fort Laramie was first established in 1834 when a group of men built a stockade to serve the needs of trappers. It soon became a stop-over for pioneers and gold panners. Its next incarnation was a station in the Pony Express and Overland Stage, finally becoming an important military post in battles with the Plains Indians.

In 1937, the Fort became a National Monument. The 22 original structures have been preserved and reconstructed to reflect the various sorts of life Fort Laramie saw. The most striking building is Old Bedlam, the oldest standing permanent military building in Wyoming. Other restored buildings include the Post's trader's store, a saloon and pool room, family quarters, cavalry barracks, guard house and bakery.

Fort Laramie is located outside Torrington in East Central Wyoming. For more information, contact Fort Laramie National Historic Site, Wyoming, 82212, (307) 837-2221.

Index

Acadia National Park 58
Air Force Museum 100
Alabama Space and Rocket Center 16
Alamo 121
Amana Colonies 49
Antietam National Battlefield 63
Assateague State and National Seashore Park 62
Atlantic City 87

Badlands National Park 115
Big Bend National Park 121
Birmingham Zoo 17
Blithewold Gardens and Arboretum 109
Block Island 110
Blue Ridge Parkway 95
Boys Town 78
Bryce Canyon National Park 124

Canaan Valley Resort State Park 136
Cape Hatteras National Seashore 95
Cape May Beaches 87
Cherry Blossom Festival 38
Cheyenne Frontier Days 139
Circus City 48
Colonial Williamsburg 129
Cooperstown 92
Country Club Plaza 75
Covered Bridge Festival 47
Cowboy Poetry Reading 82
Crater of Diamonds State Park 25

Cumberland Falls State Park 55
Custer Battlefield National Monumen 76
Custer State Park 116
Delta Queen 57
Denali National Park and Preserves 19
Diamond Head/Waikiki 40
Discoveryland's OKLAHOMA 102
Disneyland 26
Disneyworld 36
EAA's Fly-In 137
Eisenhower Center 53
Eureka Springs 24
Fall Foliage 127
Flume 85
Faneuil Hall 65
Fort Knox 54
Fort Laramie 140
Fort Moultrie/Fort Sumter 113
Garden of the Gods 28
Gateway Arch 74
Glacier National Park 19
Graceland 118
Grand Canyon National Park 21
Grand Teton National Park 139
Great Smoky Mountains National Park 119
Gulf Coast 72
Hagley Museum 34
Haleakala Crater 40
Hammersmith Farm 109
Harper's Ferry National Historic Park 135

Henry Ford Museum/
  Greenville Village 67
Historic St. Mary's City 62
Hoover Dam 22
House on the Rock 137
Independence National
  Historical Park 107
Indian Pueblo Cultural
  Center 90
International Balloon
  Fiesta 89
International Pancake
  Race 52
Iron Range Resources-
  Hill Annex Mine Tour 71
Itasca State Park/Great
  River Road 70
Jimmie Rodgers Museum 72
Johnny Appleseed
  Festival 47
Kentucky Derby/
  Churchill Downs 54
Las Vegas Strip 81
Lincoln Home 45
Little House on the
  Prairie 52
L.L. Bean Store 60
Lumberman's Museum 59
Mackinac Islands 68
McKissick Museums 114
Mississippi Belle/Spirit
  of Dubuque 50
Monterey Bay Aquarium 27
Monument Valley 21
Mt. Hood National Forest 105
Mount Rushmore 115
Mount St. Helens 131
Mount Vernon 130
Mt. Washington Cog
  Railway 84
Museum of History and
  Industry 132
Myrtle Beach 112
Mystic Marine Life Aquarium and Seaport
  Museum 30
Natchez Trace 73

National Air and
  Space Museum 133
National Old-Time
  Fiddler's Contest 42
NEBRASKAland Days 79
Nebraska State Capitol 79
New River Gorge Bridge 135
New York City 93
Niagara Falls 92
Norsk Hostfest 98
North Carolina State
  Government Complex 96
North Dakota State Fair 99
Oak Alley Plantation 57
Opryland 119
Oregon Shakespearean
  Festival 104
Ozark Folk Center
Padre Island 122
Park City Ski Area 125
Pike's Peak 29
Plimoth Plantation 64
Pribilof Islands 20
Pro Football Hall of
  Fame 100
Puget Sound Ferry 131
Rainbow Bridge National
  Monument 124
Rehoboth Beach 33
Reno National Air Races 82
Ringling Museums 35
St. Augustine City 36
St. Benedict's/Star of
  the Sea 41
Sea World 101
Sears Tower 45
Shawnee National Forest 46
Shelburne Museum 126
Silver Dollar City 74
Six Flags Over Georgia 39
Skiing/Green Mountains 127
Springs Folk Festival 108
State Fair of
  Oklahoma 103
Stone Mountain Park 38
Strawberry Banke 84
Sun Valley 43

143

Superdome 58
Tanglewood 64
Terrace Hill 49
Theodore Roosevelt National Park 98
Tulip Time Festival 68
Turquoise Trail 89
Tuskegee Institute 17
Universal Studios Tour 26
U.S. Capitol 134
Vail 28
Virginia Beach 129
Wadsworth Atheneum 30
Yale University 31
Yellowstone National Park 77
Washington Crossing State Park 88
Washington Monument 133
Washington Park 105
White River Rafting 108
White Water Rafting 43
Will Rogers Memorial 102
Winter Carnival 70
Winterthur 33
Wisconsin Dells 138

TRAVEL NOTES